WALLACE STEVENS
A World of Transforming Shapes

WALLACE STEVENS

A World
of Transforming Shapes

Alan Perlis

LEWISBURG

BUCKNELL UNIVERSITY PRESS

LONDON: ASSOCIATED UNIVERSITY PRESSES

Associated University Presses, Inc.
Cranbury, New Jersey 08512

Associated University Presses
108 New Bond Street
London W1Y OQX, England

Library of Congress Cataloging in Publication Data

Perlis, Alan, 1943—
Wallace Stevens: a world of transforming shapes.

Bibliography: p.
Includes index.
1. Stevens, Wallace, 1879–1955—Criticism and interpretation.
PS3537.T4753Z754   811'.5'2   74–19631
ISBN 0–8387–1651–2

Acknowledgment is extended to Alfred A. Knopf, Inc. for permission to quote from the following copyrighted works: *The Collected Poems of Wallace Stevens, Opus Posthumous,* by Wallace Stevens, edited by Samuel French Morse, and *The Necessary Angel,* by Wallace Stevens.

PRINTED IN THE UNITED STATES OF AMERICA

To Paula

Contents

Acknowledgments

Two Humanities Improvement Grants from Beloit College helped greatly to provide the resources for writing this book. The College has generously backed my endeavor and I am grateful for its enthusiastic support.

And I am grateful to all those who have read the manuscript at its various stages and have offered their criticism, especially to Professor James Gindin of the University of Michigan, Professor David Sanderson of Beloit College, and Professors Eva and Chad Walsh, Eva of Rockford College, Chad of Beloit. The Walshes followed the manuscript closely through all of its many transformations and their incisive suggestions penetrated the murky patches of my thinking. This book is far more precise in its style and far better organized than it would have been were it not for the Walshes's invaluable help.

Finally I would like to thank my wife, Paula. She spent many long hours listening to me read the manuscript aloud in my monotone, arresting me to challenge an idea here, a word there, and forcing me to confront some of my most sacred and fatuous notions. She kept me in a combative spirit during the year in which I had to hack away at my prose to discover the core within. Paula is the teacher behind the book, and I dedicate it to her.

I am grateful, as well, to the *Bucknell Review* for permission to quote from my article "Wallace Stevens: The Freedom to Transform" (Summer 1972); and to Faber and Faber Ltd for English-language rights for quotations from

Introduction

In the past decade Wallace Stevens has received a wealth of critical attention. Fifteen books and countless hundreds of articles have swollen the shelves of libraries. But besides the expected exegeses of troublesome passages in his poems, Stevens criticism has reflected a debilitating consistency of tone. Most critics and scholars have thus far attended to the job of "placing" Stevens in a poetical niche; but, as the poet himself has said, "The squirming facts exceed the squamous mind." The effort to catalogue the poet has left a squirming body of material unresolved.

To some degree, this is as it should be. Any poem eludes the grasp of the reader who tries to contain it. Its life is separate, a world apart from our own. And since in Stevens's many worlds there is a commensurately large population of speakers, we would have to anticipate an encyclopedia of information in order to contain them all. The facts would then have to be digested. Given that the population of Stevens's poems is nearly as varied as it is large, many critics have argued that we must recognize inherent contradictions in his philosophical premises and examine these premises individually. But the rage for order often overwhelms their argument. Herbert Stern, who among others proposes that we accept the seemingly contradictory element of Stevens's thought simply as contradictory, also contends that "there exists in Stevens's work a gradual movement in emphasis, from the commitment to the imagination *in vacuo* to a balancing concern with reality." [1] Consequently, he accuses other critics of being "guilty" of reading poems outside the context of the thrust of the *Collected Poems.*

One could write at length simply by listing the various categories under which Stevens has been subsumed. The most popular, no doubt, is his preoccupation with the tension between the real and the imagined.[2] A more recent favorite, in our existential age, is the poetry that derives from the consciousness of the "evaporation of the gods." [3] And now that New Criticism has flattened into history, we have returned to an emotive response to Stevens's poetry. Merle Brown,[4] for example, having argued that New Criticism treats poems as dead objects rather than living subjects, contends that "one must concentrate on [Stevens's] poems as physical acts bodying forth mind." Consistent with his thesis, Brown emotes for two-hundred pages, recreating the "ineffable" quality of Stevens's poems and thereby creating poems of his own, though rarely aiding in our understanding of Stevens.

It seems to me that the most successful treatments of Stevens to date have been those which have not attempted a summary of the "Whole Harmonium," but instead have concentrated on specific, noteworthy elements within individual poems and the particular issues that they characterize. Thus William Van O'Connor's pioneer book on Stevens, written while the poet was still alive, seems to ring true more than twenty years later if only because it does not formulate a single overriding synthesis that contains all the

1. Herbert J. Stern, *Wallace Stevens: Art of Uncertainty* (Ann Arbor, Mich., 1966), p. 37.

2. See Richard Heringman's essay in *The Act of the Mind: Essays on the Poetry of Wallace Stevens,* ed. Roy Harvey Pearce and J. Hillis Miller (Baltimore, Md., 1964).

3. See J. Hillis Miller's essay on Stevens as one of a number of poets whose writing stems from a belief in the "disappearance of God," in the Pearce anthology.

4. Merle E. Brown, *The Poem as Act* (Detroit, Mich., 1970), p. 37.

poems.[5] And Helen Vendler's probing study of the longer poems which, after a refreshing examination of pervasive syntactical structures in the poems, treats each one as an integral unit of thought and style, adds the, surprisingly, new dimension of close reading to the compendium of Stevens criticism.[6]

Still other critics have found in the poems a wealth of passages that link Stevens to a growing number of predecessors both by conscious emulation and by the more evasive element of history which, through either unconscious design or contact with a literary tradition, informs the poet's style and his themes. Michel Benamou's studies of the relationships between Stevens and certain French symbolist poets must, by now, be nearly exhausted.[7] And Richard Macksey, while not presuming that Stevens ever studied the work of the Phenomenologists, has pointed out several relationships between Stevens's penchant for seeing the world as a series of particulars rather than as an organic whole and the Phenomenologist's refusal to generalize from a particular body of information.[8]

We also have studies that blend Stevens's poems with his personal growth, of which Samuel French Morse's *Wallace Stevens: Poetry as Life* is the fullest and most informative. Interestingly, Morse insists that Stevens, being very much his own poet, does not lend himself to influence studies.[9] The critic contents himself with a satisfying interweaving of the poet's life, his letters, and passages from the poems,

5. I am referring here to William Van O'Connor, *The Shaping Spirit: A Study of Wallace Stevens* (Chicago, 1950).

6. See Helen Hennessy Vendler, *On Extended Wings: Wallace Stevens' Longer Poems* (Cambridge, Mass., 1969).

7. Besides a number of articles on Stevens's relationship to individual French poets, Michel Benamou has now completed *Wallace Stevens and the Symbolist Imagination* (Princeton, N.J., 1972).

8. See Richard Macksey's essay on Stevens as a phenomenological poet in the Pearce anthology.

9. Samuel French Morse, *Wallace Stevens: Poetry as Life* (New York, 1970).

thereby suggesting the directions of Stevens's growth and maturity both as a person and as a poet. What is most impressive about this book is that Morse, who is Stevens's official biographer, never tries to close off inroads to the poems. Nor does he propose a theory that wraps the poems into one neat package. Instead, he suggests directions that future critics might take, fully admitting that his own are but a few attempts to clarify issues that the general reader may find troublesome.

In what follows here, I have tried to summarize some of these issues and to reconcile others that appear contradictory. Much of this study derives from the thoughts of previous critics who have written on Wallace Stevens. Its main issue, that the poet transforms the external world that he perceives to the shape of imaginary constructs, first appeared in 1952 in an essay by Sister Bernetta Quinn. The issue has since become a popular one in Stevens criticism, but beyond Sister Quinn's brief but penetrating analysis of a handful of poems, it has never been tested in close readings. This study provides such close readings and in the process extends the range and implications of Sister Quinn's thesis.

Running seemingly counter to Sister Quinn's position is that of J. Hillis Miller and Richard Blessing. These writers concentrate less on the act of transformation that the poet undertakes in shaping the object world to imaginative demands than on the object world itself, in particular its transitory quality and what Stevens believes to be the inability of the imagination to capture it in any final form without misrepresenting it. This study attempts, through an analysis of individual poems, to reconcile these seemingly disparate views.

It would appear, of course, that the Miller-Blessing view denies the poet's ability to transform, since it precludes the opportunity for the imagination to grasp the object world in the first place. But their position relates almost exclusively to the world external to the human imagination, while Sister

Quinn's relates, with the same exclusiveness, to the world as perceived by the imaginative mind. The study that follows combines these points of view, since I believe that Stevens's most persistent effort as a poet is to combine them as well. It assumes a world in continual flux and a magician poet "capable" of changing and ordering its shapes. The motive for such a combination is Stevens's use of language, which at once provides the poet the opportunity to circle about objects and bend their shape to a variety of perspectives and to proclaim that the circling, while it "gets at" an imaginative conception of the world, fails to define the world beyond the realm of the imagination itself, or what Stevens calls the "c" of reality that precedes the chorister poet.

Such a combination of perspectives requires three indispensable elements: a notion of perception, a notion of object world, and a notion of imagination. I maintain here, as do Morse and Sister Quinn, that poetic perception is the poet's direct involvement in the object world coupled with his ability to uncover resemblances among separate phenomena within it and to communicate them as a fresh vision of an ordered whole. And, like Miller, I maintain that the object world of which the poet is a part is in a state of constant flux, and that the resemblances that the poet uncovers from within it are imaginative constructs that may satisfy the creative intellect but do not confine or define the essence of objects themselves. "The thing itself," as Stevens calls a particular phenomenon, eludes the imagination even as "ideas about the thing" proliferate. I shall expand on these Stevens-related considerations of perception and the world external to it and examine the poetic imagination as an intermediary force operating dynamically between them through the medium of language.

I shall demonstrate, for example, how the circularity and seeming repetitiousness of Stevens's language mirrors his understanding of natural processes while at the same time it tries to "tick," "tock," and "turn true" objects in the world by fitting them to imaginary shapes. Stevens as poet stalks about the world until he confines it to an imaginative center. His language is the stalking. But the world itself is protean, and the external referent that induces this circumnavigation changes utterly by the time he pins it to a state of mind. So the poet circumnavigates once again. Hence language provides an illusion of natural process while the ideas that it embodies attempt, with a futility that Stevens frankly acknowledges, to overcome natural process through transformation. I maintain here, and this is what, in the realm of theory, is unique to my study, that this paradox is the staple of his poetry and that it is in fact precisely from the tormented center, the "subtle" and ultimately inscrutable center, of the object-in-itself, object-perceived conflict that the poems secrete as vital, yet futile transformations of the object world itself.

In one of Stevens's last poems, the narrator, who sounds distinctly like the older poet himself, looks back upon his life. He sees that

> He had said that everything possessed
> The power to transform itself, or else,
>
> And what meant more, to be transformed.[10]

Natural transformation and poetical transformation are the central issues here; and for the poet, the latter is the main order of business. But why do things contain the power to be transformed? What power have we to transform them? And who is most likely to do the transforming? Many of the

10. From "Two Illustrations that the World is What you Make It" *The Collected Poems of Wallace Stevens* (New York: Knopf, 1955), p. 514. Hereafter references to the *Collected Poems* will appear, with appropriate page numbers, in the text, with the abbreviation *CP*. References to the *Opus Posthumous*, Samuel French Morse, ed., (New York: Knopf, 1958) will be abbreviated *OP*. References to the series of lectures entitled *The Necessary Angel* (New York: Knopf, 1951) will appear in the text, followed by the abbreviation *NA*.

poems disclose, as I have mentioned, that Stevens believed the world to be not only "fluent," subject of the poet's discourse, but fluid: constantly changing—growing, bearing fruit, dying, and growing again, like the human intellect. The meeting of intellect and object has in it the possibility of suggesting infinite permutations, of which the *Collected Poems* and *Opus Posthumous* contain a few. And among these permutations are connections, the parts of the world that seem, momentarily, to resemble one another in the midst of human perception before the squirming facts exceed the squamous mind. The beard becomes a river, the guitar becomes a lion's claw, the poem becomes a lion, sleeping in the sun. Stevens briefly arrests the flow of time to observe the transformations that come of resemblance. Of course the effort is no less futile than the poem is: the world proceeds to change despite imaginings. But as long as the changes take place, the mind can continue to delight in all that it is possible for it to think or say, to partake, as things appear, mature, and die, of "the pleasures of merely circulating" among them. In this book I have explored some of the reasons for Stevens's obvious delight in the act of transformation, the transformations themselves as they appear in a large number of poems, the hypothetical character of the transformer, or "hero," as Stevens imagines him, the philosophical undertones that the act of transformation suggests, and finally the landscape topography of the "imagined land," that "ultimate elegance" that emerges from the poet's vision of the world external to him. In pursuing these objectives, I have combined observations of several critics into a central issue that is far more pervasive in Stevens's poetry than previous critical evaluations have indicated. And by such a combination, I have demonstrated for the first time that the act of transformation is at the center of a number of concerns that other critics have treated individually, but never as elements that relate to one another and that cohere naturally with it.

WALLACE STEVENS
A World of Transforming Shapes

1

The Freedom to Transform

I

Every critic who has written extensively on Wallace Stevens has noted that the poet's themes are few and that his virtuoso style establishes the variety of interests that the poems suggest. The few writers who mark significant changes in the poems from *Harmonium* (1923) to *The Rock* (1955) insist that these changes concern emphasis and impact rather than a radical shift of ideas. What most impresses the reader of the *Collected Poems* and *Opus Posthumous* is that Stevens has circumvented the problem of monotony through his expansive vocabulary and his many skills as a versifier.[1] And this is the case even though, as we shall see, many of the poems consider the monotony of human life and monotony in the natural world. It is not surprising, then, that Stevens's preoccupation with the transformations that take place when the mind and nature meet reveals itself in all stages of the poet's development. For one of Stevens's most persistent contentions is that, in the realm of human perception, the

1. For an exacting and lively discussion of the richness and diversity of images in Stevens's poetry, see especially R. P. Blackmur's "Examples of Wallace Stevens," which first appeared in *Hound and Horn* 5 (Winter 1932), and was later reprinted as a chapter of his *Language as Gesture* (New York, 1952), and now appears in *The Achievement of Wallace Stevens*, Ashley Brown and Robert S. Haller, eds. (Philadelphia, 1962).

world's shape is only as constant as the mind that shapes it.

Richard Donaghue, borrowing the poet's phrase, argues that Stevens invented a "theatre of trope" in order to communicate the way the world appears under a variety of perceptual conditions.[2] His choice of metaphor is particularly apt since, according to the poet, no one phenomenon remains stable either with the passing of time or the caprice of perception. While the essential qualities of the external world may be stable, the climate in which its particulars can be found continually changes, creating a virtual theater with an infinite number of acts and a wealth of nuance. In his lecture entitled "Three Academic Pieces," Stevens explains that "the study of the activity of resemblance is an approach to the understanding of poetry. Poetry is a satisfying of the desire for resemblance" (NA, 77). Stevens has chosen his words carefully. Resemblance is an "activity" rather than simply a "phenomenon" or a "fact" because its metamorphic factor is dynamic and plural rather than static and singular. This activity is indeed theatrical.

But rather than let his prose argument stand as conclusive, Stevens supplies a poem as a kind of demonstration of his thesis: "Someone Puts a Pineapple Together." Here he writes of the "casual exfoliations" that are "of the tropic of resemblance," showing how the pineapple becomes whatever it may happen to resemble in the imagination of its perceiver.

> The momentary footing of a climb
> Up the pineapple, a table Alp and yet
> An Alp, a purple Southern mountain bisqued
>
> With the molten mixings of related things,
> Cat's taste possibly or possibly Danish lore,
> The small luxuriations that portend

2. See Donaghue's essay in the Pearce-Miller anthology.

Universal delusions of universal grandeurs,
The slight incipiencies, of which the form,
At last, is the pineapple on the table or else

An object the sum of its complications, seen
and unseen. This is everybody's world.

(*NA*, 87)

The tone of these triptychs suggests a geometrist's pro-
nouncement, a self-satisfied *quod erat demonstrandum*. The
speaker has posited a hypothetical pineapple, considered
some of its permutations as they reflect the mind of the
object's beholder, and then, like a good logician, returned to
his original object of discourse (Stevens believes that we must
always return to the real before we can begin imagining
again). As if to convince us of the ease with which such transformations take place, Stevens avoids the accessory of simile
(the pineapple, "a table Alp, is *like* an Alp") and directly unites
the object perceived with its imagined resemblance ("the
pineapple is an Alp"). One could just as easily say that an
Alp is a pineapple if it satisfied his imagination to do so.

Here we see an example of the imagination's liberty. The
poet makes no pretense of faithfully describing objects as
they exist in reality, though in other poems he toys with
the illusion of doing so. Instead, he simply makes reality
the starting point from which to explore the imagination's
fascination with resemblances. This corroborates the Quinn
point of view—with one important extension: "Someone
Puts a Pineapple Together" proposes a theory of the poetic
imagination. The object perceived is raw clay. In the poet's
mind, however, it is "bisqued," embellished, and thereby
changed by those elements of its surroundings which he con-
nects with it. The world becomes, as it were, an infinite
variety of glaze elements, from which the poet mixes the
particular concoctions that meet his imagination's satisfaction. As he applies his chosen concoction to the raw clay,
the clay assumes a transformed and distinctive quality unlike

anything that exists in reality itself, but that resides comfortably and naturally in the domain of the imagination. Every object in the world, then, is a potential analogue for every other object. The poetical mind discovers the analogues and gives them a voice, which is the articulate imagination.

Critics of Stevens are fond of remarking that the poet, through the process of analogy that I have just described, establishes a communion between the imagination and its external referent, nature.[3] If they are correct, the transformations that Stevens so often produces are merely symbols, or what T. S. Eliot calls "objective correlatives," of the poet's changing states of mind. Given this assumption, we can understand the popular view of Stevens as a symbolist poet in the manner of, among others, Baudelaire ("Nature is a living temple," a referent for the "correspondences" that take place between human and external nature).[4] In fact, however, there is little communion between the two worlds in Stevens's poetry. Monologue occurs more frequently than dialogue. The poet makes no attempt to project a sympathetic imagination into perceived objects. He would not presume to stretch either our credibility or his own "suspension of disbelief" to have us believe that the pineapple is an Alp. Like a child, he is simply at play in the fields of his own imagination, where the world is what he says it is, at least until it escapes him. But why does Stevens engage in such play?[5]

3. William Van O'Connor, for example, in a comparison between Stevens and Coleridge, remarks that "both see the imagination as a way of establishing communion with nature and enjoying it in the transformed shapes and colors the imagination makes possible." O'Connor, p. 90. And Frank Doggett has explained that the transformations that take place, "the changes of the world, are also transformations within the self." Pearce and Miller, p. 25.

4. For the most prodigious attempt to link Stevens with the French symbolist poets, see Benamou.

5. In her fine essay entitled "Metamorphosis in Wallace Stevens," Sister M. Bernetta Quinn makes the following comment on "Variations of

Perhaps because the world offers us no alternative: this, at any rate, is what the poems suggest. Stevens's early traveler, Crispin, for example, finds his world so elusive that he never resolves the question of whether "man is the intelligence of his soil" or "the soil is man's intelligence." His effort to found a local school of poets, rooted to the sense of its land, fails. As the poem concludes, Crispin is more fatalist than realist, the pudgy father of his prismy, blond daughters, the drudging husband.[6] The poem accounts for his failure.

A newcomer to the ocean, Crispin scans the space across which he plans to sail. The sea, Stevens exclaims, speaking from Crispin's point of view,

> Severs not only land but also selves.
> Here was no help before reality.
> Crispin beheld and Crispin was made new.
> The imagination, here, could not evade,
> In poems of plums, the strict austerity
> Of one vast, subjugating, final tone.
>
> (*CP*, 30)

Crispin takes the sea as an emblem of possibility, an index of the personal belief that he can see reality as it actually exists—primordial and constant, and unlike the plums that fatten, wither, and die. The "one vast, subjugating, final tone" is a persistent light in which the face of the sea never changes. It is Wordsworth's "light of common day," an aid for those who wish to see nature in a fixed and elemental state.

a Summer Day," a poem that, she argues, typifies Stevens's interest in "the fluidity of essence." "In 'Variations of a Summer Day' the rocks of the cliff are heads of dogs that turn into fishes and plunge into the sea; this, of course, happens only in the imagination though the desideratum is 'To change nature, not merely to change ideas.'" *The Sewanee Review* 60, no. 2 (Spring 1952): 244.

6. The most complete and forthright examination of Crispin's development and changes in attitude remains Hi Simons's early (1940) essay anthologized in Brown and Haller.

But we can understand, as the poem progresses, why Stevens never left the world of plums as he created an intelligence from his soil. For even as Crispin rides the sea, the world does not accept his intention.

> The earth was like a jostling festival
> Of seeds grown fat, too juicily opulent,
> Expanding in the gold's maternal warmth.
> So much for that. The affectionate emigrant found
> A new reality in parrot squawks.
> Yet let that trifle pass.
>
> (*CP*, 32)

In the "light of common day," Wordsworth's child will observe

> A wedding or a festival,
> A mourning or a funeral;
>   And this hath now his heart,
> And unto this he frames his song:
>   Then will he fit his tongue
> To dialogues of business, love or strife . . . .
>
> *Intimations of Immortality*, 11. 93–98

In such a light, Wordsworth's child will eventually view the workings of everyday life as they occur for every man. But for Crispin, that same light, which he had hoped would stabilize into a "final tone," conspires to undermine him with its "maternal warmth," keeping the world in a state of continual flux. The tone here is ironic. If Crispin must go to parrot-squawks to find reality, what is the sense of trying to locate and fix reality at all?

Finding the sun unsatisfactory to his needs, Crispin turns to the north and the moon, hoping that in the "crepuscular ice" of the Arctic he will satisfy his need for permanence. Perhaps, he thinks,

> . . . the Arctic moonlight really gave

> The liaison, the blissful liaison,
> Between himself and his environment,
> Which was, and is, chief motive, first delight
> For him, and not for him alone.
>
> (*CP*, 34)

But there is no reason to believe that the moon and Arctic twilight, any more than the sun, fix objects in their final form, or that they produce "the blissful liaison," the meeting of perceiver and object that is more than the well-turned phrase, that is the object stabilized in a form of ideal intellect. For even as Crispin imagines his voyaging to be a shuttling between transforming sun and fast-illuminating moon, Stevens loads his rhetoric with negation of such belief.

> Thus he conceived his voyaging to be
> An up and down between two elements,
> A fluctuating between sun and moon,
> A sally into gold and crimson forms,
> As on this voyage, out of goblinry,
> And then retirement like a turning back
> And sinking down to the indulgences
> That in the moonlight have their habitude.
>
> (*CP*, 35)

Such fluctuating signals the failure of the one who would hope to see the world in a single, constant light. Just as, in "Auroras of Autumn," the "scholar of one candle," the man who tries to fix the universe in stable, solitary light, stands before the shifting hues of the Aurora Borealis and feels afraid, so Crispin shrinks before the plural shapes of things that light accentuates. Yet the "indulgences/That in the moonlight have their habitude" are the workings of the imagination shaping nature to its needs. Stevens tells us "how many poems [Crispin] denied himself/In his observant progress." But this only marks him as failure rather than realist, since the shifting effulgences of the world evade the quest for fixity. Had Crispin concentrated on the poems in a potentially imaginative mind, he would not have wasted so much energy with voyaging.

We see, then, that Stevens, in "The Comedian as the Letter C," has used the sun and the moon in particular and light in general as images reflecting flux in nature. But it was not until twenty-four years later that he proclaimed, in very certain terms, the impossibility of apprehending nature as a stable realm of forms. In "Notes toward a Supreme Fiction," his thesis that the ideal poetry must be "abstract" originates from this fundamental belief. His ephebe, a young initiate into the secrets of poetry, must begin his voyage of understanding by perceiving the world as "invented" and by acknowledging that the idea of the sun is "inconceivable": it can never be finalized. With a kind of nostalgia for a simpler life in which forms existed exactly as they appeared, Stevens recalls:

> How clean the sun when seen in its idea,
> Washed in the remotest cleanliness of a heaven
> That has expelled us and our images . . .
>
> (*CP*, 381)

Without the human referent, the world is as it is. But once the human imagination enters the scene, the sharp edges of the defined world melt, and with that, the gods who signify things in their final form disappear.

> The death of one god is the death of all.
> Let purple Phoebus lie in umber harvest,
> Let Phoebus slumber and die in Autumn umber,
> Phoebus is dead, ephebe. But Phoebus was
> A name for something that never could be named.
> There was a project for the sun and is.
>
> (*CP*, 381)

The fixed embodiment of the sun, Phoebus, vanishes with the changing hues of the imagination. The project for the sun, then, is its multiple possibilities for helping in the act of transformation. It exists for us in the mind, abstracted and therefore ripe for change. Phoebus, however, is not only god of the sun, but god of reason as well, god of final understanding. His death introduces the element of unreason, or subjective and impulsive response, in the imagination. The assonantal qualities of the triptychs themselves suggest the unreason of perceiving the world as invention, or abstraction. Steven kills Phoebus twice, first in umber harvest, then in Autumn umber, suggesting thereby that Phoebus can experience his demise as often as the imagination chooses to reenact it.

Among Stevens's scattered "Adagia" one finds the aphorism: "A change of style is a change of subject" (*OP*, 171). We can see from "Notes" that Stevens means that the world is what our words make it out to be, that the sun is what we say it is, no matter how often it is mentioned. But by articulating his abstractions, the poet "bloods" them, giving the world the shape it lacks when it stands outside the purview of the imagination.

> The weather and the giant of the weather,
> Say the weather, the mere weather, the mere air:
> An abstraction blooded, as a man by thought.
> (*CP*, 385)

Later we shall observe Stevens as he creates a man out of an idea of a man. What is most significant here, though, are the terms Stevens uses to characterize the creation of metaphor—not the earth blooded, but the abstraction itself: the *idea* of the earth made flesh with words. The words of the world, then, are more real than the world itself. Here one recalls Yeats's carnate Zeus who, in "Leda and the Swan," is the "brute blood of the air," the idea of a god made flesh.

Stevens would have us believe, as he does in "Sunday Morning," that an idea made flesh satisfies our belief for final knowledge. This is why, he says, we needed to replace Jove with the living Christ, to give feet to an idea. We begin life by understanding our world as an abstraction; still restless, we give our abstraction blood.

Having argued, in part one of "Notes," that no human quest can uncover a true, unchanging world, Stevens can revolve his idea of the world as he chooses. The remainder of the poem is, among other things, a series of ideas of the world made flesh and blood as a group of mythical characters crosses the stage of the poet's imagination. Helen Vendler has already commented extensively on the significance of each member of Stevens's impressive cast.[7] I should mention Nanzia Nunzio, however, the would-be spouse who comes to Ozymandias ready to be wedded to the permanent ("standing before an inflexible/order").

> Then Ozymandias said the spouse, the bride,
> Is never naked. A fictive covering
> Weaves always glistening from the heart and mind.
>
> (CP, 396)

As if to mock her quest for permanence and order, Stevens gives his maiden the "fictive covering" of a silly and circular name, distinguished by the double gender denoted in the feminine and masculine endings. This hermaphrodite-maiden would be a hopelessly incompatible bride to the permanent. And whether or not Stevens had Shelley's Ozymandias in mind, we remember best what that king's rage for order and immortality brought him in his shattered image. The "fictive covering" is all that we can strip from the world, and at that, only to discover another fictive covering.[8]

7. See her excellent essay on "Notes toward a supreme Fiction" in *On Extended Wings*, pp. 168–206

8. Helen Vendler's comments are appropriate here. She says that "The intent of ["Notes toward a Supreme Fiction"] is not to resolve theoretical

From the thesis that the world must correspond to our image of it, Stevens moves on to declare that for the "major man," or poet—ephebe turned transformer—the world "is more fecund in principle than particle." Hence, when in the poem's final section he declares that the supreme fiction "must give pleasure," he is contemplating the poet's pleasure as well as the reader's: his delight in his own infinitely expansive capacity to alter the fleeting forms of reality to his poetical whims. This is the poet's abiding joy—"Out of nothing to have come on major weather," that satisfying shape which bloods the mind's propensities. It is our task, then, to examine some of those poems in which the delight experienced through transforming is most in evidence.

II

In his poem "Men Made out of Words," Stevens exclaims that "Life consists/Of propositions about life." This, at any rate, is the fundamental premise that guides the poet toward the act of transformation. Having examined "Men Made out of Words" closely, William York Tyndall proposes a comparison between Stevens and John Donne. He explains that "Beginning a poem with a metaphor, John Donne proceeds to elaborate it by logic. Beginning a poem with a proposition, Stevens proceeds to elaborate it by metaphor. Their procedures are not dissimilar." [9] Tyndall appears to be correct. Many of Stevens's poems are little more than hy-

difficulties but to evoke some of the hues controlling Stevens' relation to the 'untrue' mundo, as it seems from moment to moment celestial, familiar, exasperating, solacing, pleasing, and irrational" (p. 204). Ms. Vendler also remarks on the consistency of rhetoric throughout the *Collected Poems*, especially Stevens's penchant for employing the "as if" construction and thereby suggesting that the world as we see it is a system of analogues rather than a series of exclusive and fixed parts. "As if" suggests that the world is what we make it as we draw resemblances and "fictive coverings" for what we see.

9. William York Tyndall, *Wallace Stevens*, Pamphlets on American Writers, no. 11 (Minneapolis, 1961), p. 34.

potheses, or possible ways of seing the resemblance between objects—not objects that the poet finds in nature, but those that he posits from conjecture. Two poems will help to clarify the case.

"Six Significant Landscapes" is one of Stevens's earliest published poems and surely not one of his best. Its basic problem is that it resolves nothing; instead, it offers six hypothetical transformations, each serving the end of demonstrating the possibility of resemblance between seemingly dissimilar objects. While the number six here is as arbitrary as the number thirteen in "Thirteen Ways of Looking at a Blackbird," the poem itself does not build upon its initial statements; nor does it evoke the feelings of terror and helplessness so powerfully embodied in "Thirteen Ways." As an exercise, however, the poem no doubt proved helpful for the fictive master who would later make transformation a crucial factor in his poetry.

The first of these landscapes is an imitation of the style of haiku, and it reflects Stevens's youthful interest in "Chinoiserie," so popular among the imagist poets in America during the first decades of the twentieth century.

> An old man sits
> In the shadow of a pine tree
> In China.
> He sees larkspur,
> Blue and white,
> At the edge of the shadow,
> Move in the wind.
> His beard moves in the wind.
> Thus water flows
> Over weeds.
>
> (*CP*, 73)

The lines move as a series of equations: the motion of the larkspur = the motion of the old man's beard = the motion of water flowing over weeds. The old man, who blends into the shadow of the pine tree, gradually metamorphoses into water; hence symbolically he merges with the eternal flow of nature: life to death to life. But the landscape is weakened by its easy formula, which stiffens the potentially liquid grace of its movement.

The second landscape, which is less formulaic, is also more satisfying:

> The night is the color
> Of a woman's arm:
> Night, the female,
> Obscure,
> Fragrant and supple,
> Conceals herself.
> A pool shines,
> Like a bracelet
> Shaken in a dance.
> (*CP*, 73–74)

As the image of night builds, it comes to represent a female principle, fecund and sinuous. The night itself is hypothetical, "the color of a woman's arm." Slowly night and the woman combine, so that night becomes a woman's dance, a richly feminine experience, a blooded abstraction. But the poem cannot sustain its suggestive mood. Lamp posts turned into knives, long streets made chisels, domes made mallets, are at best improbable redundancies of the poem's initial premise.

More successful transformations occur in such poems as "A Rabbit as King of the Ghosts," in which the shaping light of the moon swells out the rabbit and shrinks its enemy cat, "A Primitive like an Orb," in which a cast of characters and objects are "ever changing, living in change," "Landscape with boat," in which "palms/Flap green ears in the heat," "Variations on a Summer Day," in which Stevens tells us that "one looks at the sea/As one improvises, on the piano," suggesting that the world becomes what we think it is, and the lean chant of "An Ordinary Evening in New Haven," in which the poet's attempt to reach the source of poetic truths only rips off several of the infinite layers of the fictive mask. In this late poem, the tone is resolute rather than celebratory.[10] Its persistency of meter and harsh consonance suggests a stoical affirmation of the determined will to create, stoical because, despite our search for reality, which Professor Eucalyptus claims "is as momentous as the search for God," we uncover nothing beyond our images of the world. Hence the poem affirms the dignity of the human imagination only by depicting its futility and by making that futility "noble" (one of Stevens's favorite words) through its adjunct of persistent effort. Even the whirling of the autumn leaves is an abstraction for us, rather than real motion,

Resembling the presences of thoughts, as if,

In the end, in the whole psychology, the self,
The town, the weather, in a casual litter,
Together, said words of the world are the life of the world.

(CP, 474)

Earlier in his career, however, Stevens had yet to consider the fundamental, though fruitful, hopelessness that regarding the life of things engenders in the human soul. In the early volumes, he is a "sleight-of-hand-man," often magically transforming details for the sheer delight of doing so. If a "High-toned Old Christian Woman" should present him with a pious absolute, he meets her on her own ground, in a church, and mocks her piety with fictive magic.

Poetry is the supreme fiction, madame.
Take the moral law and make a nave of it.

10. Helen Vendler's comment on "An Ordinary Evening in New Haven" is once again appropriate. She writes that the poem is "resolutely impoverished," "almost unremittingly minimal, and over and over again threatens to die of its own starvation" (p. 269). This is a bit exaggerated, perhaps, but nonetheless insightful.

And from the nave build haunted heaven. Thus,
The conscience is converted into palms
Like windy citherns hankering for hymns.

(*CP*, 59)

If the moral analogue does not satisfy the stuffy widow, the
magician has an alternative : immoral law. Take, he says,

The opposing law and make a peristyle,
And from the peristyle project a masque
Beyond the planets. Thus our bawdiness,
Unpurged by epitaph, indulged at last,
Is equally converted into palms,
Squiggling like saxophones.

(*CP*, 59)

So long as the pious widow is bound by absolutes, the
magician will transform her pieties into a musical celebration; for "the words of the world are the life of the world,"
and while the widow closes off her imagination to that frisky
world, her flagellants, severest masochists who shame themselves to reach final belief, now "disaffected," are "well-
stuffed,/Smacking their muzzly bellies in parade." They too,
like the poet, may "whip from themselves/A jovial hullabaloo among the spheres." So much for the widow, the up-
holder of absolutes. As she winces, the celebration goes on,
the palms squiggling.

Stevens's celebration of the flexibility, inventiveness, and
the sheer resourcefulness of the imagination suggests a significant question that his critics have yet to raise : does the
supremacy of the poetic imagination sustain itself in the
physical, external world? Is Stevens maintaining that the
supreme fiction is also the supreme reality, a reality of more
immediate necessity and power of revelation than the world
beyond the mind? The poems answer the question with a
doctrine of separateness, a doctrine that justifies the poet's
impulse to transform.

Stevens persistently distinguishes between "ideas about the thing" and "the thing itself." In the final poem of the *Collected Poems*, he insists on their exclusiveness. The poem's dominant metaphor is winter, with its intimations of old age and death. A nameless listener hears "a scrawny cry from outside" that "seemed like a sound in his mind." The cry and the seeming, however, are different; for the seeming cry merges and confounds with the mechanisms of dream and memories, while the cry itself, haunting the present, persists, unaltered by these mechanisms.

> That scrawny cry—it was
> A chorister whose c preceded the choir.
> It was part of the colossal sun,
>
> Surrounded by its choral rings,
> Still far away. It was like
> A new knowledge of reality.
>
> (*CP*, 534)

The poem hearkens to the comedian of *Harmonium*, who never discovers the fundamental "c," the "thing itself" that precedes the "choir" of poetic expression. But the listener of "Not Ideas About the Thing But the Thing Itself" has made that discovery and his knowledge is "new," apparently distinct from any supreme fiction that the poet confers upon reality. And since the poem is about death, Stevens is purporting that the essential "c" that precedes the choir is death itself, the only exclusively "real" thing we can know. And if death is the only reality that we can know—that we can experience as it really is instead of simply as a seeming— then the imagination, with its propensity for coloring and transforming what it perceives, takes dominion in all areas outside the realm of death while it confesses that death is our only knowable reality. The world of "ideas about the thing" is the sole habitat of the living.

An earlier poem, "Chaos in Motion and Not in Motion," justifies this argument. Its title is surely significant, for once again Stevens has divided his perspective between the object world and the perceiver. The poem concerns Ludwig Richter, "turbulent Schlemihl," who has "lost the whole in which he was contained," or lost sight of the fact that he is part of what is real. He has desires but no direction for them. As a consequence, he is "All mind and violence and nothing felt," since desire without an object of desire produces a useless, ego-centered torment. Having rejected all feelings for the object world (which here concerns other people and hence, indirectly, the theme of love), he has "nothing more to think about" and becomes a person without choices, tastes, or interests, a person wholly lacking in the powers of feeling and discrimination. He is "like the wind that lashes everything at once," he has no "ideas about the thing" and consequently he lives a life of death.

For the living, who are implicitly defined in the poems as those who have "ideas about the thing," the imagination enjoys virtual ubiquity. The poet, then, is distinctive simply because he accompanies his imaginative perceptions with a voice. In "Chaos in Motion and Not in Motion" Stevens devastates Ludwig Richter with a whimsical exercise in imaginative vision, just as he devastates the Old Christian Woman. As he meets her on her own ground, he meets Richter on his: a rainy July day. First Stevens does the looking:

> The rain is pouring down. It is July.
> There is lightning and the thickest thunder.
>
> It is a spectacle. Scene 10 becomes 11,
> In series X, Act LV, et cetera.
>
> People fall out of windows, trees tumble down,
> Summer is changed to winter, the young grow old,

The air is full of children, statues, roofs
And snow. The theatre is spinning round,

Colliding with deaf-mute churches and optical trains.
The most massive sopranos are singing songs of scales.
(*CP*, 357)

The scene at first appears chaotic, with the poet a mere spectator of random events. But at the theater of the world the poet is an active audience, cataloguing his observations and combining them in a swirl of seasonal change. In fact, the very motion of these lines defies the arbitrariness of the events they describe. Thus Stevens's vision is impressionistic rather than simply indiscriminate, and it confirms the notion that a central clay (here, a day in July) is "bisqued" in the kiln of the imagination and dappled by the facets of the world that adhere to it. The scene is indeed a "spectacle," and the poet's eye gives a spinning center to its regalia.

After presenting the mind actively engaged in propounding "ideas about the thing," Stevens can develop the profound if comical apathy of Ludwig Richter. His passive indifference, as a foil to the operations of the imagination, takes on the pale hue of death. His emptiness is as destructive of humanity's one vital concern as are the Old Christian Woman's pious absolutes. For neither character is engaged in the world of which he is a part.

Yet engagement is Stevens's idea of what is distinctly human. It defines not only a person's ability to view his world imaginatively, but also to have feelings for other people and to experience love. This perhaps explains the poet's insistence on perception as an act as opposed to a series of observations from the periphery of events. And it explains why, while in "A High-Toned Old Christian Woman" and "Chaos in Motion and Not in Motion" the personae speak with gentle mockery, in other poems of transformation their tone is more sinister. A few critics have ob-

served, most notably Samuel French Morse,[11] that Stevens
believed that poetry could provide an alternative to violence:
that the poet, unlike the self-centered, unimaginative, indifferent and therefore vicious Ludwig Richter, could, by
acting out his aggressive instincts with words, avoid physical
violence and its accompanying destruction. Despite the
accusations of the Marxist critics of the 1930s that Stevens's
rich language suggests his obliviousness to profound social
concerns like war and hunger, his poems and lectures
demonstrate acute sensitiveness to these issues. Such sensitiveness, as it is expressed in "The Noble Rider and the
Sound of Words," explains the ideal poet's role in the midst
of violence.

> Reality . . . became violent and so remains. This much ought
> to be said to make it clearer that in speaking of the pressure of
> reality, I am thinking of life in a state of violence, not physi-
> cally violent as yet for us in America, but physically violent
> for millions of our friends and for still more millions of our
> enemies and spiritually violent, it may be said, for everyone
> else.
>   A possible poet must be a poet capable of resisting or
> evading the pressure of reality of this last degree, with the
> knowledge that the degree of today may become a deadlier
> degree tomorrow.
>
> (NA, 26–27)

As a statement pertaining to the avoidance of reality, this
typifies Stevens's exclusive faith in the imagination. The way
the poet resists violence in the world is by exhausting his
instinct for violence in poetry, which becomes a moral
alternative to war, an outlet of the sort William James might
suggest. Hence Stevens's transformational poems not only
consider violence, but frequently express themselves violent-
ly. For example, Stevens's lion in "Poetry is a Destructive

11. Morse, p. 77.

Force" and elsewhere is akin to Blake's tiger, since it is the fleshing out of human violence as well as an image of its own.

> That's what misery is,
> Nothing to have at heart.
> It is to have or nothing.
>
> It is a thing to have,
> A lion, an ox in his breast.
> To feel it breathing there.
>
> Corazon, stout dog,
> Young ox, bow-legged bear,
> He tastes its blood, not spit.
>
> He is like a man
> In the body of a violent beast.
> Its muscles are his own . . .
>
> The lion sleeps in the sun.
> Its nose is on its paws.
> It can kill a man.
>
> (*CP*, 192–93)

One could read this poem simply as a statement of the possible dangers inherent in the written word. In any event, in the poem it is more important to note the destructive power of poetry than it is to note the destructive power of the lion. This lion lives in the human breast, is latent, perhaps, but always in a position to strike with its claws.

And strike it does, especially in "The Man with the Blue Guitar," even though the destructive force is thinly veiled with the strum of a musical instrument. Helen Vendler has perceptively considered "Blue Guitar" as a "duet with the undertaker," a counterpointed instrumentation of poetry and death.[12] As the poem depicts the guitarist playing "things as

12. Vendler, pp. 119–44.

they are," he uses his transforming propensity to rip away
the curtains from the stage of the human imagination for
the sake of revealing its inner workings.

> The person has a mould. But not
> Its animal. The angelic ones
>
> Speak of the soul, the mind. It is
> An animal. The blue guitar—
>
> On that its claws propound, its fangs
> Articulate its desert lays.
>
> (CP, 174)

The animal within us claws its song onto the page, shaping
reality to its sometimes violent will. To accentuate this
proposition, Stevens writes explosively, sounding more like
a voodooist than "man number one," his ideal of a poet.

> Ah, but to play man number one,
> To drive the dagger in his heart,
>
> To lay his brain upon the board
> And pick the acrid colors out,
>
> To nail his thoughts across the door,
> Its wings spread wide to rain and snow,
>
> To strike his living hi and ho,
> To tick it, tock it, turn it true,
>
> To bang it from a savage blue,
> Jangling the metal of the strings . . .
>
> (CP, 166)

The effort, here, is to make and dissect a man, by clawing
on the strings of a guitar to reveal man as he is, pinned and
naked. The savage delight that the poet takes in this act,

however, fails to produce anything but an abstraction, since the world moves faster than the brutal image of it picked out on the guitar. This does not mean, though, that the guitarist fails to produce a man. Indeed, he succeeds; but the man he creates is a hypothetical man, the newest incarnation of an ancient myth.

As such, he is a testament to the power of the imagination and its facility in the act of transformation. The modern man, clawed open from his source in myth, emerges:

> From this I shall evolve a man.
> This is his essence: the old fantoche,
>
> Hanging his shawl upon the wind,
> Like something on the stage, puffed out,
>
> His strutting studied through the centuries.
> At last, in spite of his manner, his eye,
>
> A-cock at the cross-piece on a pole
> Supporting heavy cables, slung
>
> Through Oxidia, banal suburb,
> One-half of all its installments paid.
>
> Dew-dapper clapper-traps, blazing
> From crusty stacks above machines.
>
> Ecce, Oxidia is the seed
> Dropped out of this amber-ember pod,
>
> Oxidia is the soot of fire,
> Oxidia is Olympia.
>
> (CP, 181–82)

In his own typical way, Stevens, who here most fruitfully compares to Donne, disguises illogic with the mask of metaphor, gradually transforming Christ to modern man, crucified on the electric poles of his invention. The fulcrum of the canto is the word *slung*, which bridges the original cruci- fixion and the condition of suburban man. The initial man that the by-now-frantic guitarist "evolves" is a "fantoche," a marionette, an invention. He has been invented before, and the guitarist merely needs to re-create him in the image in which he so often appears, hung along a cross-piece. But is this man, this mythical Christ, any less of an abstraction than the citizen of Oxidia? No, claims the guitarist, who strings mythical man across the centuries to a grimy, credit- run world and gives him his ignominious second coming. Oxidia is the soot from the same fire that once burned in Olympia, where Hephaestus shaped his own machines.

The process here is clear: posit a man, give him flesh, place him in a context. Soon enough, as the next canto shows, he will have an argument with his employer. Begin- ning with an abstraction and giving it concretion, Stevens seems to have created a man more "real" than any to be found in fact. The act of transformation, a phenomenon of the mind that sees the world slip by too quickly to be held, claws together another world quite visible enough for most men's tastes. But "The Man with the Blue Guitar" concludes on a softer note, the guitarist having exhausted himself with his frenetic songs.

> The bread
> Will be our bread, the stone will be
>
> Our bed and we shall sleep by night.
> We shall forget by day, except
>
> The moments when we choose to play
> The imagined pine, the imagined jay.
>   (*CP,* 184)

In time the guitarist will posit still another world—when nature, by its elusiveness, reminds him of all that the mind can invent. In the meantime, has he not touched us in our world with his imaginings?

In a poem written thirteen years after he completed "The Man with the Blue Guitar," Stevens summarized the power of poetry as "A freedom revealed, a realization touched,/ The real made more acute by an unreal." In this wholly neglected poem, "The Bouquet," the real is so touched by the unreal that, besides becoming more acute, it becomes even more elusive than it does elsewhere in the *Collected Poems*.

The poem deals with "meta-men and para-things." If we take the prefix *meta* to mean "along with," "between," "among" or "akin," the "meta-man" is a man among men, the type of man that Stevens calls a poet in "Esthétique du mal." A "meta-man" is also a maker of metaphors. If we take the prefix *para* to mean "at the side of" or "secondary to," "para-things" refer to things imagined from, or created in addition to, the real. "The Bouquet" meets both definitions as it considers the situation of reality from the eye of the poet. For, regarded by the "meta-men," the bouquet is "quirked/And queered by lavishing of their will to see."

As in "Notes toward a Supreme Fiction," Stevens begins "The Bouquet" by establishing as his setting "a land/Without a god." There, someone sees a duck swimming on a lake —not directly, though, but through a doorway. But even as Stevens toys with the image of the duck by blurring our vantage point, he increases the difficulty of perception by concentrating on the duck's wake, a thing that changes with motion, an "image spreading behind it in idea." The green bouquet apparently stands in the doorway, since it "comes from the place of the duck" (or is the duck merely fecund in a singular way, giving strange birth likely to take place only through Stevens's wizardry?). At this point, we have an image of the shifting of reality: the bouquet can be observed only against a changing background.

Once again, however, Stevens multiplies perceptual pos-

sibilities, continuing to move outward from his initial focus,
like one walking back from an object, all the time holding
a camera to his eye. He notices the cloth covering the table
on which the bouquet stands. Then his eye

> fastens intently to these lines
> And crawls on them, as if feathers on the duck
> Fell openly from the air to reappear
>
> In other shapes, as if the duck and tablecloth
> And the eccentric twistings of the rapt bouquet
> Exacted attention with attentive force.
>
> A pack of cards is falling toward the floor.
> The sun is secretly shining on a wall.
> One remembers a woman standing in such a dress.
>
> (*CP*, 450)

Once Stevens tells us that the bouquet is "rapt," we believe
that after many hesitations and backward steps he has merely made a transference from the imagined to the real. The
bouquet is "rapt" (pun on "wrapped?") because it exists in
the mind. Twice more he shifts his focus, however, and
finally he mentions that "one remembers a woman standing
in such a dress." Is the scene we have just observed—lake,
duck, bouquet, and table—an imprinted image on a dress?
The participial form of the verb, used throughout the des-
criptive section of the poem, suggests just such an eternal
present. And yet the "checkered squares" of the tablecloth
"breathe slightly" with the motion of the woman's body:
stasis in motion. Only the imagination could conjure such a
feat.

But as if to tell us that the imagination's hold on its own
perceptions is tenuous, Stevens adds still another scene to
the poem.

A car drives up. A soldier, an officer,

Steps out. He rings and knocks. The door is not locked.
He enters the room and calls. No one is there.

He bumps the table. The bouquet falls on its side.
He walks through the house, looks around him and then leaves.
The bouquet has slopped over the edge and lies on the floor.
(CP, 452–53)

How is it possible that a bouquet that is printed on a dress
can be knocked over? It appears that Stevens has simply
absorbed the printed scene into his mind and given it an
epilogue, as we might do to a novel that ends inconclusively.
The shift from iambics to near prose in this final section
suggests a stage direction as a conclusion to the poem:
enter an officer (a soldier, who stands in opposition to the
"meta-men" and who is a figure who would presume to
order reality), who knocks over a bouquet, the poet's original
center of observation. Once the bouquet has fallen, the scene
itself collapses about it. The poem ends. For the imagination,
as the poet tells us, this clawing lion, is a "finikin thing of
air." Since we have no recourse from such things in a com-
prehension of reality, however, this "finikin thing" is our
humble, human excuse for understanding.

<h1 style="text-align:center">III</h1>

The urge to transform that emerges so often in Stevens's
poetry suggests an internal struggle in the poems between
the natural and the unnatural. While every critic of Stevens
mentions conflicts in the poems between things real and
things imagined and between the quotidian and the exalted
life of the imagination itself, none has suggested that these
conflicts themselves derive, in good measure, from Stevens's
tendency to balance that which human hands and minds
evolve and that which exists untouched in its natural element. Stevens wrote several poems expressive of this elemental tension.

"Anecdote of the Jar," which is one of this number, has received more critical attention than any other poem among Stevens's works. Suffice it to say here that one of its crucial points is that the jar, while it may reflect the hill on which it stands and therefore represents a work of art, is not nature, since it is barren ("It did not give of bird or bush"). Once nature is reflected, it is art—the domain of the imagination and not of the real world. The phenomenon of reflection produces the same theme in a later poem, "The Glass of Water."

> Here in the centre stands the glass. Light
> Is the lion that comes down to drink. There
> And in that state, the glass is a pool.
> Ruddy are his eyes and ruddy are his claws
> When light comes down to wet his frothy jaws.
> (CP, 197)

By now the lion is a familiar figure in Stevens's poems. Here it once again stands for the potentially violent imagination, temporarily in a state of calm. The glass, placed in the center of nature, is the human mind caught, for the sake of hypothesis, in a fixed position. First it observes light, next the lion, as things pass by its reflecting surface. Hence Stevens has created an illusion of nature transforming itself, as it does on the jar in Tennessee. But the poem's final stanza undercuts the illusion. For fat Jocundus, the poem's character, is less interested in mind as glass than he is in the living mind.

> But in the centre of our lives, this time, this day,
> It is a state, this spring among the politicians
> Playing cards. In a village of the indigenes,
> One would still have to discover. Among the dogs and dung,
> One would still have to contend with one's ideas.
> (CP, 198)

In reality, one's mind is active rather than fixed. Even as one stands on his native soil, he still must make it part of his intelligence. Though the mind cannot, literally, "give of bird or bush," it ultimately has only itself to contend with as it transforms fleeting images from nature to meet its own demands.

But as Stevens celebrates the "jovial hullabaloo" that the transforming mind can concoct, he recalls that nature, so alien to human concerns, constitutes a threat to those concerns. For example, when the speaker of "In the Clear Season of Grapes" thinks of the land,

> I think of the house
> And the table that holds a platter of pears,
> Vermilion smeared over green, arranged for show.
>
> (*CP*, 110)

But he knows that this careful arrangement, a contrivance, would be "a flip for the sun and moon" to produce with their light. Nature, the speaker realizes, means more than what the mind can draw from it. And the forms in nature mean far more than "a flip for the sun and moon."

> . . . they do.
> And the mountains and the sea do. And our lands.
> And the welter of frost and the fox cries do.
>
> Much more than that. Autumnal passages
> Are overhung by the shadows of the rocks
> And his nostrils blow out salt around each man.
>
> (*CP*, 109–10)

As we imagine painted pears, real foxes circle us with their breath, reminding us that nature persists despite our efforts to contain it in the forms of art. In "Thirteen Ways of Looking at a Blackbird" Stevens asks:

O thin men of Haddam,
Why do you imagine golden birds?
Do you not see how the blackbird
Walks around the feet
Of the women about you?

(*CP*, 93)

While, as the guitarist in "Blue Guitar" explains, "Franciscan don was never more/Himself than in this fertile glass," he is himself only until he dies, at which time nature will absorb him into the reality he could never fix in life.

What appears to be curious about "In the Clear Season of Grapes" is that the poem never mentions grapes. But this is precisely its point: for us, the arrangement of pears could just as easily be an arrangement of grapes. Our subject is what we make it. In the imaginative mind, the tension between nature as it exists and nature as we wish it to exist is resolved through the act of creation. Stevens's poems embody such a resolution, while the poet entertains himself with fictive coverings, knowing he can have no more than fictive coverings. But his action is often desperate, like the frantic clawing on the blue guitar. If we realize that, despite ourselves, the fox's "nostrils blow out salt around each man," we begin to understand the poet's giddy desperation.

2

The Noble Rider: Poet as Hero

> To say more than human things with human voice,
> That cannot be; to say human things with more
> Than human voice, that, also, cannot be;
> To speak humanly from the height or from the depth
> Of human things, that is acutest speech.
>
> (*CP*, 300)

A distinguishing mark of most great poets is that they create whole mythologies rather than separate, unrelated poems. Dante and Blake are perhaps the most obvious examples; but there are scores more. Either through the epical treatment of a hero's life, the repeated treatment of a single character or image, or the preoccupation with a single theme or set of themes, they embrace a mythical and complex world. Stevens's poems display this distinctive mark in each of the categories I have mentioned. His traveler Crispin appears many times in the poems in different guises, but he is always trying to grasp some essential center that he maintains each object or phenomenon possesses. Stevens frequently introduces a previously successful image in a new context to show how objects are colored by their surroundings. And he revivifies the triptych innumerable times to test the nuance of a phrase. Such is the effort of the poet who wishes to be known for his work rather than for his isolated poetic accomplishments.

In the previous chapter, we have observed that one of Stevens's most persistent traits is his use of metaphors that undergo transformations as the poems in which they occur proceed. I have attributed this trait to his belief that the imagination, bereft of any hope to discover the true, the final reality, is free to pursue its own translation of what it perceives. To accomplish this position, however, the poet must experience the futility of his ignorance and persevere in the midst of flux by writing the words that please his inner calling. In Stevens's complex mythology, such a poet is called "hero," or "major man," and he struggles against a force variously named Ananke, or necessity, or nature, a force unfathomable though often threatening.

But before we can examine the role of the hero in Stevens's poems, we must set him in relation to his antagonist, nature. Since Stevens does not hold faith in any effort to comprehend or re-create the essence of nature, we may be led to expect that he believes nature itself to be an illusion, or at best an imperfect reality that the poet, by a monumental effort of the mind, "methodizes" or makes perfect. Such is not the case, however. He is neither Platonist nor Neoclassicist. Indeed, his most recurring exclamation is that "I am myself a part of what is real, and it is my own speech and the strength of it, this only, that I hear or ever shall" (NA, 60). The poet-hero must recognize that he is a part of a broader reality, that his very existence proves that we live in a world of fact and not illusion, and that any poet who would deny such fact could be nothing more than an inventor of fairy tales. Among the poets who have conceived of themselves as nature's lover, Stevens, who calls the world "my green, my fluent mundo," must be ranked as one of the most ardent.

But he loves a dumb presence. Nature has no voice of its own. If it is fluent, it is because poets have given it speech and an intelligence. When Stevens exhorts us that we must continually turn to what is real, he means that we must give reality that "subtle centre" which makes it mean in human terms. After denying to the day-dreaming woman in "Sunday Morning" the "imperishable bliss" that she seeks, Stevens reminds her that

> We live in an old chaos of the sun,
> Or old despondency of day and night,
> Or island solitude, unsponsored, free,
> Of that wide water, inescapable.
> Deer walk upon our mountains, and the quail
> Whistle about us their spontaneous cries;
> Sweet berries ripen in the wilderness . . .
>
> (*CP*, 70)

From such a statement we would anticipate a simple affirmation of the presence of a palpable reality. But Stevens also tells us that "A poet's words are of things that do not exist without words" (*NA*, 32). What we perceive in nature, then, is incommunicable without the aid of language. Nature meets our demand for understanding only when, with words, we localize it in our intelligence.

We might say that Stevens's poems, taken together, embody a philosophy of metaphor and, through this philosophy, suggest a way that we might accommodate ourselves to a world that is beyond our understanding. But here one must distinguish between Stevens and his romantic predecessors. As Elizabeth Sewell has convincingly argued, the romantic impulse, as it extends from the effort to unite consciousness with external nature, is to conceive of a marriage between these two forces. Using *The Prelude* as her example, she notes that when Wordsworth considers how "the discerning intellect of man" is "wedded to this goodly universe/In love and holy passion," he is contemplating a uniting of the human spirit with a spirit already suffused through nature. The marriage of the mind and the external world, she concludes, is seen no longer as the domination of one by the other, but the interpenetration of two systems, who are to achieve their "blended might"—in contrast to the mind subjugating nature, and, one surmises, much more healthily, whether in interpretation of the universe or in the institution of marriage—something which the poet calls creation.[1]

The word *system* suggests an order in nature consistent with the romantic tendency to observe a spirit pervading it; for Stevens, on the other hand, the poet alone can discover order in nature, but only through the appropriate arrangements in the imagination. He celebrates no weddings,[2] but instead marvels at what the mind can conceive from its random impressions, of which human life is one. It would be impossible, then, for Stevens's poet to achieve an understanding of nature through "recollection in tranquility" or through "wise passiveness." Only the active mind, confronting nature's raw materials, can shape them to form and then, through transformational metaphors, make that form meet the needs of the inspired imagination. As to finding a permanent force in nature that gives it its own order, Stevens has an appropriate response:

> And yet what good were yesterday's devotions?
> I affirm and then at midnight the great cat
> Leaps quickly from the fireside and is gone.
>
> (*CP,* 264)

It is precisely nature's evasiveness that gives the poet the freedom to transform. Hence, while Wordsworth's growing child in Book II of *The Prelude* is "creator and receiver both,/Working but in alliance with the works/Which it beholds," Stevens's ephebe must develop awareness by perceiving "this invented world," which, as we have seen, exists in the mind.

1. Elizabeth Sewell, *The Human Metaphor* (South Bend, 1964), p. 82.
2. Indeed, he denies Nanzia Nunzio her wedding to the permanent in "Notes toward a Supreme Fiction."

Such a position with respect to the external world demands a definition of reality that would be alien to Stevens's romantic predecessors. He writes that:

> The subject matter of poetry is not that "collection of solid, static objects extended in space" but the life that is lived in the scene that it composes; and so reality is not that external scene but the life that is lived in it. Reality is things as they are.
>
> (NA, 25)

The imaginative mind, then, like the jar in Tennessee, is a focal reflecting point; situated in reality, yet unlike other objects in reality capable of perceiving it, it makes human sense out of an otherwise indifferent world. When in *Biographia Literaria* XIV Coleridge remarks that the poet is an unusual member of his society because, unlike his fellow members, he has keen powers of observation and notices objects that others might ignore, he suggests that the objects themselves contain the power of revealing themselves. When in *The Necessary Angel* Stevens remarks that the poet explores "The life that is lived in the scene that it composes," he suggests that any life outside of human interaction with it constitutes an inchoate and speechless mass. Stevens's poet can never simply be a recorder; he is always a transformer.

To fit nature to the human need is a prodigious task. It demands far more than keen observation. It demands as well unflagging inventiveness and enough flexibility to make new devotions each day. Stevens calls the person who can accomplish such devotions "hero," and he garlands him with praise for the reach of his imagination. He is a major figure in the poems. Indeed, he is on Stevens's stage far more frequently than any other of his characters. Given the poet's absorption in the process of transformation, the hero's ubiquity is inevitable. It is he, after all, who, recognizing nature's elusiveness when he stands outside it and sensing

the need to transform it when he stands within, is the
necessary angel of a disordered world inhabited by man.

II

In "Paisant Chronicle" Stevens distinguishes between the
common man and the "major men," or heroes. Initially he
outlines the ordinary ideals by which people live: their
desire for bravery, their faith in human endurance, their
need for admiration—a whole chronicle of human endeavors.
These people are part of the sum of what Stevens calls "reality." But beyond such ordinary humanity live the "major
men."

> The major men—
> That is different. They are characters beyond
> Reality, composed thereof. They are
> The fictive man created out of men.
>
> (*CP*, 335)

The fact that the fictive man is "created out of men" rules
out any possibility that he either evolves from or is inspired
by a divine presence. If he is a sort of superman it is because he is so much of his place and time that he is their
quintessence. His is a very public voice. As such, the fictive
man can be found only in an ordinary setting:

> But see him for yourself,
> The fictive man. He may be seated in
> A café. There may be a dish of country cheese
> And a pineapple on the table. It must be so.
>
> (*CP*, 335)

"It must be so" since this extraordinary man becomes the
hero because he is so fully a part of what is real. One recalls
here Carlyle's characterization of the "hero as poet" as a
man brooding over the world from a position of exile, pain-

fully observing what he has lost. So much a part of his world that he personifies it, Stevens's poet-hero could never live at such remove. He is central in his place.

He lives in this world, Stevens tells us, because there is no place else for him to go. What he observes on the table, changed by his perception as it may be, consists of the finest presences he can know:

It is possible that to seem—it is to be,
As the sun is something seeming and it is.

The sun is an example. What it seems
It is and in such seeming all things are.

Thus things are like a seeming of the sun
Or like a seeming of the moon or night

Or sleep. It was a queen that made it seem
By the illustrious nothing of her name.

Her green mind made the world around her green.
The queen is an example . . . This green queen

In the seeming of the summer of her sun
By her own seeming made the summer change.
(*CP*, 339)

Here the hero poses as heroine, the same heroine who "sings beyond the genius of the sea" in "The Idea of Order at Key West." Stevens works toward an almost transcendental position since he depicts a reality that one must swoop through and beyond in order to realize its final significance. These lines, indeed, show a clear progression in a meditative process.[3] They work from the seeming world, which comprises the outer limit of human perception, to the seeming world

3. See Louis Martz's essay "Wallace Stevens: The World as Meditation" in the Boroff anthology.

as epiphenomenon of mind, to mind itself now green (taking on nature's hues), to mind, supreme fictive master, mastering the world by making summer change. This process occurs within the spiraling tones of the couplets as well as in their presentation of mental activity. If this poem, as the title indicates, is "Description without Place," it is so only because place has been transformed into mind, which becomes a complex diamond mirroring the facets of the universe to ordered form. As the poem later announces, "Description is revelation." The green queen, more than symbol of fertility, is birth, life, death, and place itself, the local haunt of what occurs within the universe. As such, she is infinite possibility and ultimate shaper. And as heroine, she is someone in whom others can believe. As Stevens puts it in his essay "Two or Three Ideas," "it is for the poet to supply the satisfactions of belief in his measure and in his style" (OP, 206).

In the poems the movement toward the affirmation of the hero frequently occurs in the same way. Even as they assert placelessness, they begin with a "local habitation and a name." "I placed a jar in Tennessee," "I sang a canto in a canton." But the effort to affect place always concludes with a voice that has sung through place to understanding, changing the shape of place along the way. For example, when the listener-lover in "On the Road Home" assents to the argument that there is no absolute truth in nature and therefore knows that she can move beyond it, it is then that

> the silence was largest
> And longest, the night was roundest
> The fragrance of the autumn warmest,
> Closest and strongest.
>
> (CP, 204)

We can sense nature most when, being part of what is real, we transcend it by realizing its intimate character in the mind.

Such an act receives Stevens's most profound admiration. For it exposes the human being as total—intellectually acute and intensely physical. The intellectual aspect of the heroic act, the act of localizing nature in the mind, is forcefully expressed in "The Idea of Order at Key West." The mysterious heroine, no more presence than the voice of a poem, is one of Stevens's most respected makers.

> For she was the maker of the song she sang,
> The ever-hooded, tragic-gestured sea
> Was merely a place by which she walked to sing.
> Whose spirit is this? we said, because we knew
> It was the spirit that we sought and knew
> That we should ask this often as she sang.
>
> (*CP*, 129)

We ask to know the spirit of the singer because we know the answer. It is the soul and intellect of man. The heroine's song which, we later discover, transforms the sea across which it sails as a boat does with its wake, affirms our capability for mastering our world: "the sea/Whatever self it had, became the self/That was her song." [4] But these lines also suggest that the heroine is evanescent: she has no shape beyond that which the human will for belief in the self invests her with. While Carlyle argues [5] that the poet-hero's writings are the consummation of a force or sentiment that has gained power through the centuries, Stevens argues that

4. Robert Pack argues that in Stevens's poems "the quality of a perceived object becomes part of the quality of the perceiving imagination," which leads to a "desired unity of person and place." Robert Pack, *Wallace Stevens: an Approach to his Poetry and Thought* (New York, 1958), p. 65.

5. As Carlyle says of the poet-hero, "All past inventive men work there with him;—as indeed with all of us, in all things." See *Carlyle's Works*, vols. 1 and 2 (Chicago, 1889), 1: 326. In his poem "Chocorua to its Neighbor," Stevens proclaims that the hero is the collective will of humanity: "He came from out of sleep./He rose because men wanted him to be" (*CP*, 299).

the poet-heroine's song is the collective will of humanity realized in a single, encompassing sentiment. So pervasive, indeed, is this argument that the poems usually present it with the same syntactical formula: "beyond . . . yet of themselves." [6] Such is the position of the hero as he asserts his shaping intellect.

But since the hero must be a part of what is real, we must observe him in his physical activities as well. Often, Stevens portrays him as a Dionysian reveler, chanting his transparent song of place into the sun. This physical hero takes center stage in "Credences of Summer," a poem in many ways similar to "Sunday Morning" although written some thirty years later.

The poem begins with a conventional invocation to celebration typical of the pastoral mode. But the beginning is even more typical of the Stevensian mode of hypothesis. "This is the last day of a certain year," he tells us, "Beyond which there is nothing left of time." In the life of the imagination, time can stop long enough for the grasping of essential fact. We can "postpone the anatomy of summer" if not arrest it forever. In this hypothetical state, Stevens urges us to "see the very thing and nothing else./Let's see it with the hottest fire of sight." We must grasp reality "without evasion by a single metaphor" in order to reach the "centre" that we seek. Like "Sunday Morning," "Credences of Summer" establishes an atmosphere in which we can experience final belief, an ultimate grasping of the universe, a glimpse of "green's green apogee." Like Keats's "Ode on a Grecian Urn," the beginning of this poem fixes time at a moment of rich growth.

But Stevens is obviously self-conscious about the conventions with which he is working. He asks us to "say" that "this is the centre which I seek," fully aware that discovering it is an impossibility. For just as he essays to complete his

6. Or, as in "Paisant Chronicle," " beyond . . . composed thereof."

hypothetical scene, he adds new details to it, cognizant that the scene he has thus far depicted is "too ripe for enigmas, too serene," and too austere for a poet's touch of nuance. The summer day, which he has tried to rip from time, now becomes part of the larger reality of a year.

> The more than casual blue
>
>> Contains the year and other years and hymns
>> And people, without souvenir. The day
>> Enriches the year, not as embellishment.
>> Stripped of remembrance, it displays its strength—
>> The youth, the vital son, the heroic power.
>>
>> (*CP*, 375)

The summer day cannot stand alone, even in the poet's imagination. It is only a part, though like all other parts a forceful one, of the broader reality in which it stands.

Having thus established that today's growth is part of tomorrow's fruition, Stevens can introduce his Dionysian hero, a celebrant of time's perpetual motion and nature's continual change. Since the poem focuses on a pastoral celebration, however, Stevens gives the scene the fanfare of a revelry. The hero is a complex of the celebration rather than the solitary celebrant.

> Far in the woods they sang their unreal songs,
> Secure. It was difficult to sing in face
> Of the object. The singers had to avert themselves
> Or else avert the object. Deep in the woods
> They sang of summer in the common fields.
>
> They sang desiring an object that was near,
> In face of which desire no longer moved,
> Nor made of itself that which it could not find . . .
> Three times the concentered self takes hold, three times
> The thrice concentered self, having possessed

The object, grips it in savage scrutiny,
Once to make captive, once to subjugate
Or yield to subjugation, once to proclaim
The meaning of the capture, this hard prize
Fully made, fully apparent, fully found.

(CP, 376)

Here one is reminded of the "ring of men" in "Sunday Morning" who "chant in orgy of a summer morn" naked among the gods. They are "like a savage source" and, like the celebrants of "Credences of Summer," grip objects with a "savage scrutiny" while trying to win the root at their center. The celebrants in "Credences of Summer," however, sing of the "common fields" while they stand "deep in the woods." In other words, they affirm the supremacy of the imagination by imaging one world while standing in the midst of another. What is more important, though, is that they carry out the same meditative process that the heroine in "Description without Place" does, first grasping the object under observation, next capturing it, or localizing it in the imagination, and finally subjugating it, or making it a permanent part of the human domain.

The process in which this ring of celebrants engages changes the whole focus of the poem. Now Stevens no longer needs to arrest time, to see nature momentarily fixed and therefore unreal. Once the heroes have grasped their "hard prize" in the mind, they can invoke nature to continued evolution and change:

Fly low, cock bright, and stop on a bean pole. Let
Your brown breast redden, while you wait for warmth.
With one eye watch the willow, motionless.
The gardener's cat is dead, the gardener gone
And last year's garden grows salacious weeds.

(CP, 377)

The "salacious weeds" are emblems of change, and perhaps death, and the collective hero who later springs from them is the mirror of this shifting summer scene. Suddenly the speaker no longer feels self-conscious about the pastoral mode in which he is expressing himself. The "youthful happiness" with which the poem concludes is an indication of a conciliatory mood. The summer festival, like nature, can proceed to develop and alter itself because the reality that the hero has grasped with "savage scrutiny" has been shaped to the imagination's need and has therefore satisfied the urge for final belief despite the external phenomena of change.

In each of the poems we have thus far considered, the hero, regardless of the sensual intimations of his presence, is essentially bodiless. He is a sort of invisible Aeolian Harp, through which a chaotic wind sweeps into beautiful melody. But it is finally the melody that speaks to us of nature transformed and not the hero himself. As Robert Pack explains, "The hero lives only in our imaginations, in our poems, and it is there that we meet and know him." [7] But what is still more significant is that the hero, like nature itself, is something we move through on our way to belief. When in "Asides on the Oboe" Stevens proclaims that "the prologues are over," that we must now consider "final belief," and that final belief "must be in a fiction," he uses his hero as the glass through which we can perceive this final belief.

> It was not as if the jasmine ever returned.
> But we and the diamond globe at last were one.
> We had always been partly one. It was as we came
> To see him, that we were wholly one, as we heard
> Him chanting for those buried in their blood,
> In the jasmine haunted forests, that we knew
> The glass man, without external reference.
>
> *(CP, 251)*

As the glass man chants for the dead, he expresses our sorrow as well as his own. He is complete, "without external

7. Pack, p. 156.

reference," because as he sings he embodies all that matters in the human mind. He is our collective soul.

This is a theme that appears often in Stevens's poems. In "Montrachet-le-Jardin," he acknowledges the presence of the hero only because the hero is man and "man must become the hero of his world." And in "Examination of the Hero in a Time of War," he argues that we need to believe in the hero because he is like us and not greater than us. Unless we believe in the hero, Stevens exclaims, we cannot believe in ourselves. But it is crucial to realize that, for Stevens, the hero reflects our "best self," as Matthew Arnold puts it, and not our "ordinary self." As heroes, we are always "capable," transforming nature to an imaginary ideal that corresponds to belief. Since capability is not concrete, however, we cannot make images of the heroic potentialities within us. Hence, in "Examination of the Hero," Stevens denounces the effort to mold heroism to shape. Heroism, he says,

> is not an image. It is a feeling.
> There is no image of the hero.
> There is feeling as definition.
> How could there be an image, an outline,
> A design, a marble soiled by pigeons?
> The hero is a feeling, a man seen
> As if the eye was an emotion,
> As if in seeing we saw our feeling
> In the object seen and saved that mystic
> Against the sight, the penetrating,
> Pure eye. Instead of allegory,
> We have and are the man, capable
> Of his brave quickenings, the human
> Accelerations that seem inhuman.
>
> (CP, 278–79)

A statue of a hero is less than human, a marble debasement of our capabilities. An idea of a hero, on the other hand, is humanity at its best.

But what is humanity at its best? Since it is the hero, since the hero is the ideal poet, and since poetry ideally fashions nature to a human need, humanity at its best is a collective creative force unwilling to fix nature in a permanent conception and consequently unwilling to rigidify itself in absolute belief. We are beginning to observe that for Stevens, like Arnold, poetry not only expresses the "best self" of the poet, but that it is a "criticism of life" as well. Indeed it might be Arnold's voice instead of Stevens's that we hear when the latter proclaims: "After one has abandoned a belief in God, poetry is that essence which takes its place as life's redemption" (*OP*, 158). And it is very close paraphrase to "The Function of Criticism at the Present Time" when Stevens insists that "It is life we are trying to get in poetry" (*OP*, 158). In trying to reflect humanity at its best, Stevens's poems are most emphatically a "criticism of life."

A large majority of his hero poems appear in two volumes: "Parts of a World" and "Transport to Summer." Most of these poems were written during World War II, when Stevens suffered the anguish of war with the vision of a man of peace. Many times over the poems affirm the bounty of the heart and condemn the brutality of the heartless man. Hence his image of the hero splits in two: on one side stands the war hero, who achieves recognition by murder; on the other side stands the heart's hero, who pierces through reality to find a belief that transcends and dissipates the attitudes of war. As Northrop Frye explains, "Just as there is false metaphor, so there is false myth. There is in particular the perverted myth of the average or 'root man' [Montrachet-le-Jardin] . . . the genuine form of the war-hero is the 'major man' [Paisant Chronicle] . . . who . . . is personified as peace, the direct opposite of the war-hero." [8]

8. Northorp Frye, "The Realistic Oreole: A Study of Wallace Stevens," Boroff anthology, p. 171.

To the "best self" ideal, the average man, who is capable of waging war, is a frightening aberration.

One of the reasons he is so frightening is that he is heartless. In "Extracts from Addresses to the Academy of Fine Ideas," Stevens considers his hollow sentiments :

> Thus
> The maker of catastrophe invents the eye
> And through the eye equates ten thousand deaths
> With a single well-tempered apricot, or, say,
> An egg-plant of good air . . .
>
> (*CP*, 253)

We have seen that for the poet-hero, nature must be abstract. But he must never consider man as an abstraction, for if he is perceived as such, he becomes expendable. Thus Stevens defeats the war hero with the force of rhetoric, reducing him and then elevating him to major man, poet projected into a state of fact.

> ". . . If,
> Against the edge of ice, the abstraction would
> Be broken and winter would be broken and done,
> And being would be being himself again,
> Being, becoming seeing and feeling and self,
> Black water breaking into reality."
>
> (*CP*, 255)

Once again the hero's heart beats with the fluid of his veins : he is too much a part of reality to escape it through insidious abstractions.

Stevens's facile annihilation of the war hero suggests that he has faith in a fundamental human goodness. Hence he regards the violent revolutionary, Konstantinov, who appears in "Esthétique du Mal," as an illogical maniac in a world that survives through the logic of the perceiving imagination.[9]

9. In chap. 1 we examined Stevens's contention that the perceiving

One might meet Konstantinov, who would interrupt
With his lunacy. He would not be aware of the lake.
He would be the lunatic of one idea
In a world of ideas, who would have all the people
Live, work, suffer and die in that idea
In a world of ideas. He would not be aware of the clouds,
Lighting the martyrs of logic with white fire.
His extreme of logic would be illogical.

(CP, 325)

In these lines, Stevens abandons the iambic foot that governs the rest of the poem. Often, when he wishes to reinforce an important point, he lapses into prose statement, retaining only the process of metaphor to indicate his statement's fitness to the poem as a whole. Here the argument follows the premise that despite the cruel machinations of the illogically violent, unnatural man, there remains a powerful impulse within all of us to be ourselves, "the unalterable necessity of being this unalterable animal." Even the tragedy of war, Stevens tells us, can be turned into the gaiety of peace when we express our best self, which is a part of what is real:

The tragedy, however, may have begun,
Again, in the imagination's new beginning,
In the yes of the realist spoken because he must
Say yes, spoken because under every no
Lay a passion for yes that had never been broken.

(CP, 320)

It is within the context of reality that we possess the freedom to transform, to affirm the power of the imagination. But we

imagination is governed by unreason. The only way to reconcile this contention with Stevens's attitude in "Esthétique du Mal" is by suggesting that the imagination's unreason has its own self-contained logic that combats the illogical mania of those who, like Konstantinov, would reduce human beings to inflexible abstractions and thereby render them expendable.

are not at liberty to shape the destiny of man from without.

What is perhaps most real for Stevens is the human heart, whose pulse figures in the framework of the external world. The hero is a heart-filled man, nature's companion and its rightful artificer. It is therefore the hero to whom Stevens gives the privilege of defeating, in very emphatic terms, the man of war.

> Thence came the final chants, the chants
> Of the brooder seeking the acutest end
> Of speech: to pierce the heart's residuum
> And there to find music for a single line,
> Equal to memory, one line in which
> The vital music formulates the words.
>
> Behold the men in helmets borne on steel,
> Discolored, how they are going to defeat.
>   (*CP*, 259)

In what Stevens calls "an age of disbelief," language becomes the incarnation of the highest aspirations of the human soul. And the hero, forceful and "capable," is the bringer of life's "redemption": poetry, which is a term for love.

III

One of the reasons that Stevens denounces the men with the steel helmets is that they embody the spirit of negation. Renouncing the real world in favor of abstractions, they embrace the dangerous notion that things external to the mind can be absorbed into the mind and thereby stripped of their sovereignty. They perpetuate the illusion that nature is subject to human control and that the way one "solves" the universe is to fix it with the intellect and suppose that he has fixed it in unchanging fact. This, for example, is the position in which Mrs. Alfred Uraguay finds herself when she says:

> "I have said no
> To everything in order to get at myself.
> I have wiped away moonlight like mud. Your innocent ear
> And I, if I rode naked, are what remain."
>
> *(CP, 249)*

As if to respond to such rejection, to the frank negation of things real, "The moonlight crumbled to degenerate forms." For, as Stevens explains, "Her no and no made yes impossible." Her attempt to find absolute truth has blocked her access to the imagination, where the only truths, the mind's translations of phenomena, can be revealed. In the quixotic world of Mrs. Uraguay, however, there is always the hero, the noble rider "intent on the sun" and "capable," who redeems the world by virtue of his presence in it. Like a victor, he emerges from the skeletons of negation to hear a world that rings with intensest sound.

> The villages slept as the capable man went down,
> Time swished on the village clocks and dreams were alive.
> The enormous gongs gave edges to their sounds,
> As the rider, no chevalere and poorly dressed,
> Rode over the picket rocks, rode down the road,
> And, capable, created in his mind,
> Eventual victor, out of the martyr's bones,
> The ultimate elegance: the imagined land.
>
> *(CP, 249–50)*

The night, which is silent for Mrs. Uraguay because she negates it, erupts in a burst of sound for the noble rider, because he will fashion an imagined land from what he hears. The earth, once martyred to the mood of Mrs. Uraguay, now springs to life again.

In this poem, Stevens toys with an old cliché. The paradigm of revelation is the person who climbs a mountain in search of truth. Reaching the summit, he sees before him an expanse, a perspective, a totality that he may understand as realization or truth. Mrs. Alfred Uraguay is such a climber, gradually stripping away her garments, or embellishments, to face the naked truth. But the hero of the poem is the man who descends the mountain and rides into the midst of fact. Perhaps he is as inelegant as Mrs. Uraguay is elegant; but unlike her, he knows that the world cannot be understood from outside and that no single fact can stand in isolation from its context. As Stevens argues, "An isolated fact, cut loose from the universe, has no significance for the poet. It derives significance from the reality to which it belongs" (OP, 235). As such a poet, this noble rider yokes his world to the transparent glass that is his mind, himself shoddily but fully dressed.

The situation of the noble rider is a Stevensian ideal, and it is one that many of his fictive personages seek to emulate. Among these is the soldier who speaks to us in "Repetitions of a Young Captain." He is a refinement of an earlier Stevens character, the baffled speaker in "Metaphors of a Magnifico," who postulates and then rejects various analogies to the scene that he observes. Ultimately the magnifico, a flustered eccentric, realizes that his metaphors will not "declare" themselves as truth. At the conclusion of the poem he remains where he began, contemplating a handful of details with which he cannot reconcile himself. Unlike the magnifico, however, the young captain gradually senses something of significance in what he sees. If he does not discover truth, at least he uncovers the meaning of the search for truth, which Stevens suggests is one of the few goals that the hero can achieve.

We gather from the poem's beginning that the captain, while overseas and in the midst of war, has experienced an event, possibly the one that he narrates, that has been traumatic for him. Having returned to America, he realizes that the event has lost its clear edges in the time-warp of memory. By recreating the event in his mind, however, he hopes to separate present from past by giving memory meaning and purpose. Once he sat in a theater, watching a performance, when a violent wind ripped away its roof. Nevertheless,

> The people sat in the theatre, in the ruin,
> As if nothing had happened. The dim actor spoke.
> His hands became his feelings. His thick shape
>
> Issued thin seconds glibly gapering.
> Then faintly encrusted, a tissue of the moon
> Walked toward him on the stage and they embraced.
> (*CP*, 306)

The roof of the theater denotes a protective covering from reality. Its ruin enables nature and the human drama on the stage to unite. Suddenly, in a typically Stevensian motif, a fiction takes its place at the center of what is real. A stage light is replaced by moonlight.

The captain, though, is a long way from comprehending the significance of his recollections. First he must locate them in some identifiable past time and separate them from the common lot of men of war who, in their brutality, reveal a "make-matter, matter-nothing mind." Out of his memories, the young captain must fabricate something that matters. Otherwise, he will be doomed to repeat the tragedy of his past, a past that includes killing in the name of pious abstractions.

The captain learns to separate past from present—something that the magnifico does not learn—by ruminating on his own condition, by fitting time to memory. He comes to understand that "The departing soldier is as he is./Yet in that form will not return." Having come back to America, the captain has entered a new reality that affords new opportunities for understanding. What he hopes to accomplish in his new environment is a total change of consciousness from a war mentality to a peace mentality. He uses the destruction of the theater as the pinpointed index of this change, since it stands for the annihilation of all human abstractions, for the explosion of the theater locked within itself. Now he finds a metaphor that corresponds to his new role as part of what is real. He calls it "the organic consolation":

> the complete
> Society of the spirit when it is
> Alone, the half-arc hanging in mid-air
>
> Composed, appropriate to the incomplete,
> Supported by a half-arc in mid-earth.
> Millions of instances of which I am one.
>
> (*CP*, 309)

The captain sheds the egotism of the man of war, whose concocted self-elevation "makes him rise above the houses, looking down." [10] and realizes himself as part of the general community of man. Like that of other sincere men, his spirit is a "half-arc" that finds its complement in "mid-earth." Willing to join nature, since both nature and the human spirit are devoid of sense when isolated from each other, he can achieve the posture of the hero in his finest moment.

> The choice is made. Green is the orator
> Of our passionate height. He wears a tufted green,
> And tosses green for those for whom green speaks.
>
> Secrete us in reality. It is there
> My orator. Let this giantness fall down
> And come to nothing. Let the rainy arcs
>
> And pathetic magnificences dry in the sky.

10. Stevens treats this imaginary self-enlargment playfully in the more jocular poem "A Rabbit as King of the Ghosts."

Secrete us in reality. Discover
A civil nakedness in which to be.

In which to bear with the exactest force
The precision of fate, nothing fobbed off, nor changed
In a beau language without a drop of blood.

(*CP*, 309–10)

The young captain has won an education in the world of
green. He can reduce the man of war to human size, reject
pretense; secreted in reality he finds the words that join the
two halves of the arc and finds the means for disengaging
the savage spirit from the urge for war. Moreover, he has
acquired the ability to transform; taking the real world as
his referent, he has shaped a consciousness of peace. And
he has taught us that transforming from the world of fact
is accepting human fate: the peaceful way to survive in a
world that continually changes its face.

The captain's heroic victory signals a pervasive theme in
all of Stevens's major poems written after World War II:
constant meditation on the world of objects brings with it a
self-understanding in the human spirit. This is a theme that
Stevens follows with heroic, almost stoical determination in
"An Ordinary Evening in New Haven"; for here, Stevens
must contend with the real, with the object world, at its
most banal and insignificant level. And yet he must call
what he learns a revelation, even if that revelation is "a
shade that traverses/A dust, a force that traverses a shade."

For what Stevens insists upon, in canto after canto of
"Ordinary Evening," is that the capable man, even "in the
midst of foreignness," must make the world a part of himself, indeed so much a part that its "confused illuminations
and sonorities" are "ourselves" and "we cannot tell apart/The
idea and the bearer-being of the idea." The endpoint of
"perpetual meditation" is the union of the man and his
ideas: philosopher and philosophy as one, the man wholly

himself. Stevens persistently exclaims that the imagination, projected into the real world, not only colors and transforms what we see, but comes to inform and embody the identity of the imaginer himself. His heroic voice modulates the world in "paradisal parlance," and for him,

> The sun is half the world, half everything,
> The bodiless half. There is always this bodiless half,
> This illumination, this elevation, this future
>
> Or say, the late going colors of the past,
> Effete green, the woman in black cassimere.
> If, then, New Haven is half sun, what remains,
>
> At evening, after dark, is the other half,
> Lighted by space, big over those that sleep,
> Of the single future night, the single sleep,
>
> As of a long, inevitable sound,
> A kind of cozening and coaxing sound,
> And the goodness of lying in a maternal sound,
>
> Unfretted by the day's separate, several selves,
> Being part of everything come together as one:
> In this identity, disembodiments
>
> Still keep occurring. What is, uncertainly,
> Desire prolongs its adventure to create
> Forms of farewell, furtive among green ferns.
>
> (CP, 481–82)

Once again, we find the joining of two halves corresponding to the union of the real world and the imagination. But here the joining takes place at a still point of creative fulfillment and death. We are reminded of Marvell's bird which, in his poem "The Garden," is a symbol for the human soul gliding through the green world and coming to rest on the branch of a tree, "wetting its wings for final flight." [11] The heroic

11. Robert Buttel also finds a similarity between Stevens and Marvell

realization that everything can "come together as one" becomes the hero's epithet, his grasp of meditative complete-
ness and the rounding out of his identity.

In *The Collected Poems* only two figures emerge as
having achieved this ultimate state of being. One is George
Santayana, whom Stevens praises in "To an Old Philosopher
in Rome." The other is Stevens himself who, in the highly
autobiographical volume "The Rock," is mythologized into
an archetypal old poet looking back upon and estimating
his life. In "To an Old Philosopher," which Randall Jarrell
believed to be Stevens's greatest poem,[12] Santayana stands
"on the threshold of heaven," from which vantage point
the objects of this world shrink to insignificance. He has
achieved the "celestial possible" (what Stevens calls "paradisal parlance" in "An Ordinary Evening"), a condition in
which all things—"The bed, the books, the chair, the moving
nuns"—are a part of his self. Hence "each of us/Beholds
himself in you, and hears his voice/In yours." The hero,
absorbing the voices of the universe, becomes the universal
voice, the identity in which all men can behold themselves
because it reveals all human concerns. Since Stevens does
not believe in a heaven, however, he can only allude, at the
poem's conclusion, to the heavenly state in which Santayana
resides. "He stops on the threshold" of life and death

> As if the design of all his words takes form
> And frame from thinking and is realized.
>
> (*CP*, 511)

He has developed a complete identity—an identity that is

in their mutual affirmation of the meditative process in which the mind,
sweeping through nature, alights to find itself fully realized: "Annihilating
all that's made/To a green thought in a green shade." Robert Buttel. *The
Making of Harmonium* (Princeton, 1967), p. 201.

12. See Jarrell's impressionistic but interesting rankings of Stevens's
poems in his review of the *Collected Works*, which can be found in Brown
and Haller.

an imaginative mirror of the external world—in which all men can discover meaning.

In a world of continual flux, this is the only identity that is permanent. In "The Poem that Took the Place of a Mountain," Stevens contemplates how he has "shifted the rocks and picked his way among the clouds" in order to bring the whole world into his purview, to mold the chaotic world to a system outlined by the imagination, all the time maintaining that world's sovereignty. At last he would discover a view toward which the things of this world "edged," a permanent reality that would survive examination by the contemplative mind. His work then complete, himself established, he could lie in peace "and, gazing down at the sea,/ Recognize his unique and solitary home." That home is the identity that the old poet has established for himself. For this heroic man, having transformed his world, having affirmed the right to human life in the face of war "in a beau language without a drop of blood," and having enclosed the world in his identity, thereby making himself identifiable to all men—a model of nobility, has touched the greatest height a man can reach in this most mortal world.

3

Round and around: Poetry and Futility

The temptation to link Stevens's poetry to a philosophical system is very great. The reader emerges from the *Collected Poems* having sensed that the poet articulates a distinct position both with respect to the operation of the human imagination and to the relationship between thought and external nature. Having encountered a good deal of the meaning of what Stevens says in the work of other writers, he wishes to place the writer in a philosophical framework that harks back to a body of speculative thought previously proposed and to insert the poet into the history of ideas.

Some of the earliest Stevens criticism considers the question of whether or not the body of his work bears the stamp of "philosophical poetry." In 1945 Hi Simons, perhaps one of Stevens's most astute critics because he usually did not feel compelled to establish the poet's position in the history of thought, tried to dispel the controversy by outlining the major philosophical tenets of the poems and thereby to propose their "genre." [1] While his outline indicates four significant frames of thought that appear in the poems, it does little to show how these frames are distinc-

1. Hi Simons, "The Genre of Wallace Stevens," in the Boroff anthology, pp. 43–53.

tive; indeed, the major proposition of the essay is that Stevens's poems recall a metaphysical tradition exemplified by Donne. Simons simply fails to give Stevens a voice of his own.

Simons's essay appears to have opened a floodgate to let out a wash of proposals linking Stevens to various literary and philosophical figures. Those proposals which have confined themselves to isolated elements within the poems that have overtones of a preestablished philosophical position have for the most part successfully proved that Stevens did not write in an intellectual vacuum, that he is part of an American tradition in literature, and that, being human, he naturally reflected basic human preoccupations in his writings.[2] Other proposals, however, have collected the poems under the umbrella of a single philosophical position.[3] In these essays, one senses that the impulse of the writer is to say "Stevens is a metaphysical poet," or even more specifically, "Stevens is an existentialist" or "Stevens is a phenomenologist."

Richard Macksey's consideration of phenomenological elements in Stevens's poetry is a case in point. He argues that Stevens, like the phenomenologists, aspires to see objects objectively, to understand them as they exist in nature, uncolored by the imagination. Moreover he contends that Stevens, in proper phenomenological fashion, concentrates on particulars without relying on the falsifying machinery of generalization to make his poems mean. According to Macksey, Stevens's theatricality reflects a marvelously varied circus of phenomena arrested by the poet's discerning eye

2. Especially Samuel French Morse and Roy Harvey Pearce. See the Pearce anthology. Pearce has done the most to place Stevens within an American tradition of literature, particularly in his essay entitled "The Life of the Imagination," which Marie Boroff has anthologized, pp. 111–32. Joseph Riddel's comparative study of Stevens and Whitman (Boroff, pp. 30–42) is quite helpful in localizing Stevens's position within the tradition.

3. See Macksey's essay, also J. Hillis Miller's on "The Disappearance of God," both in the Pearce anthology.

and brought to the reader with a voice that is the speaking mechanism of that eye. Yet while his thesis is imaginative, his overall position is insubstantial in two crucial ways. First, it suggests that Stevens's theoretical empiricism that is part of his view of nature (which is only a means toward reaching the transformational position we examined earlier) is an off-shoot of phenomenology. Yet it might just as well be connected to nineteenth-century logical positivism or to the thought of Matthew Arnold who, like Stevens, makes the proclamation that the purpose of poetry is "to see things as they really are." [4] Second, while phenomenology is not the original philosophy of particulars, it is the most outspoken in refusing to connect particulars and to contrive syntheses; it abdicates point of view, or inclusive position, in favor of microscopic observation and exclusive vision. Yet Stevens continually argues that an object, to be properly perceived, must be beheld in relation to its environment. Thus far, the fictive product of the phenomenological point of view has been a fragmented series of incidents or observations void of a consistent narrative position; it is up to the reader to make connections and to order information sequentially. Stevens's poems, on the other hand, invariably reflect a narrative point of view and a sequential presentation of images.

Macksey's argument, then, suggests some of the dangers inherent in trying either to connect Stevens's poems to a philosophy or to call Stevens himself a philosopher. Yet we have already observed that Stevens articulates a rather distinctive position toward the connection between mind and the external world, which enables him to transform what he sees to special poetical shapes; and we have also observed that he creates the heroic figure who engages in such a shaping process. We would perhaps like to associate Stevens with his contemporaries, with Pound, Eliot, and

4. This is Arnold's prevailing thesis in "The Function of Criticism at the Present Time."

Yeats, for example, and say that his tendency to present his ideas symbolically, with symbol as part of the logic of a given poem rather than merely its embellishment, places him squarely in the tradition of literary modernism. In fact, however, the poems of the modernist tradition are for the most part anti-heroic in point of view and indifferent to the problem of establishing the relationship between the human mind, or human creations, and external nature. And unlike the poems of Stevens, they are more concerned with individual consciousness than they are with establishing a sense of place.

In fact, much in Stevens's poems seems almost anachronistic. His belief that the ideal poet should be a hero of his age harks back to Ruskin and Carlyle and their insistence that the creator's sentiments, his monumental presence, can be felt with a proper sense of his creations. And his concern for the way nature should be portrayed in literature is a footnote to a controversy that raged throughout the nineteenth century but had nearly disappeared by the beginning of the twentieth.[5]

The debate among poets over the proper representation of nature in literature was most intense during the romantic period, when the poets were involved in formulating a personal identity that corresponded to activities in the natural world. By the middle of the nineteenth century John Ruskin had emerged from this debate as the principal spokesman for the position that nature did not possess human attributes and that it was only through the operation of the imagination that nature became a "companion to man." He argued against Wordsworth's popularizers by attacking the poet's "morbid" preoccupation with what he thought was a sentimental notion that nature contained its own humanity. Thirty years ago, in a very useful study, Josephine Miles traced the decline in use of the "pathetic fallacy" over a

5. Josephine Miles considers this debate in detail in her book *Pathetic Fallacy in the Nineteenth Century* (Berkeley, Calif., 1942).

period of one-hundred years and attributed this decline to a growing awareness that nature, contrary to the claims of the romantics, was a detached and empirically knowable, if not fixable, presence.[6] Stevens's poetry stands as an afterthought to this awareness.

Ruskin's anti-romantic feelings are most in evidence when he discusses the pathetic fallacy. He writes that "The temperament which admits of the pathetic fallacy," which confers human attributes on insensate objects, is

> that of a mind and body in some sort too weak to deal fully with what is before them or upon them; borne away, or over-clouded, or over-dazzled by emotion; and it is a more or less noble state, according to the force of emotion which has induced it.[7]

The emotional states that Ruskin most often found connected to the pathetic fallacy, however, were ignoble; "the curious web of hesitating sentiment . . . and wandering fancy which form a great part of our modern [i.e., romantic] view of nature." [8] Stevens nearly echoes Ruskin's argument, differing from his predecessor only by sounding unequivocal in admitting no nobility to the emotions inspiring the use of the pathetic fallacy. He contends that we must "somehow cleanse the imagination of the romantic."

> The imagination is one of the great human powers. The romantic belittles it. The imagination is the liberty of the mind. The romantic is a failure to make use of that liberty. It is to the imagination what sentimentality is to feeling. It is a failure of the imagination precisely as sentimentality is a failure of feeling. (NA, 138)

Both writers are eager that the feelings expressed toward external nature recognize both the sovereignty of nature it-

6. Miles.
7. *Modern Painters* 3, Pt. IV, chap. 12, paragraph 8.
8. *Ibid.*, chap. 13, paragraph 13.

self and the sovereignty of the imagination. Only then, they believe, can we comprehend nature as it is, with the detachment that admits of its changing face. It is precisely their admiration of inanimate objects that makes them give greatest value to the objects themselves and less to their suggestion of a human situation or their tendency to arouse sentimentality. As Stevens explains, "the more intensely one feels something that one likes, the more he is willing for it to be what it is" (*OP*, 175).

Ruskin's influence on poetry and poetic theory was very strong through the last four decades of the nineteenth century. He was writing contemporaneously with the English positivists, and this must have helped to give respectability to his essay on the pathetic fallacy in particular and his attack on romantic sentimentality in general. By the 1880s writers had become self-conscious about being overly sentimental and adamant in arguing that nature was dumb except as it spoke with the voice of man.[9] Hopkins in particular reflects this self-consciousness and speaks firmly to his belief that nature communicates only with the aid of a human voice. In "Ribblesdale," for example, he proclaims:

Earth, sweet Earth, sweet landscape, with leavès throng
And louchèd low grass, heaven that dost appeal
To, with no tongue to plead, no heart to feel;
That canst but only be, but dost that long . . .

And what is Earth's eye, tongue, or heart else, where
Else, but in dear and dogged man.

9. Here Josephine Miles's study is most helpful, since it counts the frequency of occurrence of the pathetic fallacy in the writings of the poets from the romantic, Victorian and modern periods. Her statistical conclusion is that decline in frequency over a period of one hundred years is nearly two hundred percent. She attributes this decline in particular to Ruskin's criticism and in general to the growing belief that sentimentality expressed in praise of nature is an index of the inaccurate and unobjective eye of the observer.

Once and for all, Hopkins gives primacy to the imagination, to the human propulsion of nature into communication. By the turn of the century, the debate over how nature should be presented in literature had died to a whisper. Only the critics remained to pick it apart and discover its crucial elements, to give it a fixed place in history. When we think of that debate today, we think of its scholars rather than its poets; we recall Frederick Bateson,[10] Cleanth Brooks,[11] Joseph Warren Beach,[12] William Empson,[13] and John Crowe Ransom,[14] all of whom during the 1930s wrote important studies of the position of nature in English and American poetry. By that time, poets had begun to turn inward, to move from external phenomena to states of mind. And the journey into consciousness left little time to consider the apparels of Mother Nature.

But even as late as the 1940s Stevens was unearthing the old debate, insisting, in "Notes toward a Supreme Fiction," that the gods in nature had died and that the poet must regard "things as they are" if he is to portray nature sincerely and give it the attributes necessary to enable us to understand it. It was in the 1940s that Stevens, giving a nod to the pragmatism of William James, declared that "the truth that we experience when we are in agreement with reality is the truth of fact" (*NA*, 59). And sounding like a Shelleyan in defending the supremacy of poetry and like a Ruskinian in affirming the intimate relationship between poetry and factual truth, Stevens also declared that "when men, baffled by philosophic truth, turn to poetic truth, they return to their starting point, they return to fact ..." (*NA*, 59).

10. F. W. Bateson, *English Poetry and the English Language* (Oxford, 1934).
11. Cleanth Brooks, *Modern Poetry and the Tradition* (Chapel Hill, N.C., 1939).
12. Joseph Warren Beach, *The Concept of Nature in Nineteenth-Century English Poetry* (New York, 1936).
13. William Empson, *Some Versions of the Pastoral* (London, 1935).
14. John Crowe Ransom, *The World's Body* (New York, 1938).

We could continue to discover poets, critics, and philosophers whose notions clearly resemble Stevens's. The number of analogues to any person's thoughts is most likely enormous, and Stevens himself is fond of remarking that the poet puts new clothes on old ideas because new ideas are so rare. What is more interesting is that, in two important ways, Stevens's own poetry leans back in time to preoccupations that had long since disappeared. The crucial problem for the critic, though, is to come to terms with the way these two prominent issues in Stevens's poetry—his concept of the hero and his notion of the way nature must be perceived in order to be transformed to the satisfaction of the imagination—meet and fuse to shape a prevailing attitude toward life that speaks through the poems.

II

As a poet, Stevens felt that he expressed himself "in the intricate evasions of as" while trying to "get at" the center of reality through the process of metaphor. I have already noted his fondness for positing hypotheses as a means of elaborating on his central themes. These hypotheses can be seen as conceits, each one an example of the point of view the poems in which they occur put forth. One fact stands secure in the critical canon collecting about Stevens's poems : the singular focus and solitary theme of every individual poem. That even the longer poems circumvent the problem of monotony indicates the tremendous degree to which Stevens relied on metaphor and hypothesis, on elaboration, to keep his poems vital and dynamic despite their limited range of ideas.

For it is elaboration, or the edifice and surrounding filigree of language, that mediates the object world and the world as perceived and that, for critical purposes, resolves the seeming conflict between the Quinn view of transformation and the Miller-Blessing view of the inaccessible world of things. For Stevens, language provides the illusion of re-producing objects and actions in external nature while in fact language transforms them from one circumstance to another: being-in-nature to being in the mind, which alone is capable of perceiving resemblances. The circularity of Stevens's language, its tendency to bend back upon itself, seems to imitate (though as I shall argue, it cannot mirror) the cyclical process of natural events, while its repetitious-ness seems to imitate recurring patterns in natural phe-nomena. The crucial issue here is that of illusion, since the poet's mimetic efforts are the stuff of language and structure and not of nature's muteness and "chaos in motion." Lan-guage is simply different from nature, though it evolves from it and in some instances seems to imitate it. Hence poetry cannot capture elements in the object world, as both Miller and Blessing argue, but it can, as Sister Quinn argues, transform them in the mind. In fact, the impulse to trans-form, for Stevens, is rooted precisely in the poet's inability to capture the world and render it in its own condition. What is perhaps unique to Stevens is that the poet's failure is cause for celebration.

"An Ordinary Evening in New Haven" is no doubt the most obvious case in point. The central issue of "Ordinary Evening" is the attempt to characterize a place, to localize reality and say, with confidence and finality, that New Haven lives and is epitomized in the poem. That the poem ends inconclusively with respect to its stated objective in-dicates the futility one experiences in discovering that the "getting at"—the act of poetry—is never finalized. Nothing is ever totally known. Since the "getting at" is our only available resource in our quest for knowledge, however, the poem moves forward with variations on its theme even though its message never changes. Ultimately, "Ordinary Evening" is a gigantic monument of words containing a solitary message, which has been turned and tempered by the poet's supple voice. Like a grain of sand in an oyster, the poem's theme acts as an irritant that stimulates secretion of a larger verbal substance.

Stevens achieves this growth of form around theme by circulating about his subject and adding one or two verbal signposts as he turns. The effect is magnetic, as if each revolution about his subject attracted an original facet to an old idea and made it appear new. As Stevens puts it: "Metaphor creates a new reality from which the original appears to be unreal" (OP, 169). In expressing the intimacy between place and state of mind in "Ordinary Evening," Stevens relies on this circularity, or what he calls "endless elaboration," to demonstrate that man is the intelligence of his soil.

In the land of the lemon trees, yellow and yellow were
Yellow-blue, yellow-green, pungent with citron sap,
Dangling and spangling, the mic-mac of mocking birds.

In the land of the elm trees, wandering mariners
Looked on big women, whose ruddy-ripe images
Wreathed round and round the round wreath of autumn.

They rolled their r's there, in the land of the citrons.
In the land of big mariners, the words they spoke
Were mere brown clods, mere catching weeds of talk.

When the mariners came to the land of the lemon trees,
At last, in that blond atmosphere, bronzed hard,
They said, "We are back once more in the land of the elm trees,

But folded over, turned round." It was the same,
Except for the adjectives, an alteration
Of words that was a change of nature, more

Than the difference that clouds make over a town.
The countrymen were changed and each constant thing.
The dark-colored words had redescribed the citrons.

(CP, 486–87)

This is perhaps the most complex and involuted canto in "Ordinary Evening," since several processes occur simultaneously. The language turns back on itself, rolling its r's and its m's. Tones repeat themselves, though the words in which they occur slant away from one another ("dangling and spangling," "round and round the round wreath"). Each line elaborates the one that precedes it by adding a nuance of color or a single detail. Yet the canto ends where it began, in the land of the citrons.

As if to complicate matters, Stevens has the mariners end their journey where they began as well. They pick up new details at each pass in their circular trip. Moreover, the activity described in the canto is an analogue to the poetic process of circulating—"But folded over, turned round." Yet the canto collects as it circles, adding adjectives, just as the mariners collect images as they circle, gradually coming to create the intelligence of the soil in the land of the citrons, where the citrons themselves are colored by the mariners' experiences.

Meanwhile, the poet tells us many crucial things: that adjectives transform the world to the demands of the imagination, that "a change of style is a change of subject," that the soil is man's intelligence (the mariners are "bronzed" by their "blond atmosphere") and that a turning is a shaping that gives a location to central meaning and collects the nuances that sustain the excitement of the poem. Since we never fully comprehend the land of the citrons, we can only "turn it true": substitute imaginative truth for what we cannot isolate and know as fact.[15]

One might be tempted to conclude that Stevens's word-play, his tendency, for example, to bring a single syllable to a crescendo, is merely an embellishment of what might otherwise be a terser, more direct statement. A. Alvarez has been Stevens's most outspoken critic in condemning the

15. A lesson that Crispin should have learned before setting out on his journey.

poet for his paucity of subject matter and for a reliance on style and figure of speech to fluff out a poetry that might well communicate its meaning in a more condensed fashion.[16] What Alvarez has neglected, however, is that, far from embellishment, Stevens's verbal fusillade is the meaning of his poems itself. The poet makes this point in several poems in *Harmonium* and sustains it throughout his career. Peter Quince explains:

> Just as my fingers on these keys
> Make music, so the selfsame sounds
> On my spirit make a music, too.
> Music is feeling, then, not sound.
>   (*CP*, 89–90)

If we accept the proposition that music and the musical elements of poetry affect the spirit in the same way, we can only conclude that poetry, too, is feeling as well as sound; that poetry can make our being "throb/In witching chords" and at the same time be an incarnation of the poet's feelings. In this way, mellifluous sound becomes an integral part of a poem's message, without which the poem would be lifeless and inflexible.

That circularity is so basic a part of Stevens's tonal system indicates his reliance on it as a vehicle of feeling. And "Peter Quince at the Clavier" is only one of many poems in which this circularity modulates into musical motifs. "Evening without Angels," for example, is an orchestra of lutenists with the poet as its conductor. Even as the poet rejects the human tendency to project gods into a mortal world and angel-lutenists into the clouds, so he conducts his argument in "an accord of repetitions": strings plucked steadily to articulate the rhythms of our man-bound earth. While the wind is "encircling us" and speaking "always with our speech," the poet spills out his desire.

16. A. Alvarez, *The Stewards of Excellence* (New York, 1958).

... Evening, when the measure skips a beat
And then another, one by one, and all
To seething minor swiftly modulate.
Bare night is best. Bare earth is best. Bare, bare,
Except for our own houses, huddled low
Beneath the arches and their spangled air,
Beneath the rhapsodies of fire and fire,
Where the voice that is within us makes a true response,
Where the voice that is great within us rises up,
As we stand gazing at the rounded moon.

(*CP*, 137–38)

The poem eliminates angels from this world only to elevate
the human soul to an angelic height. It does so by spiraling
downward in a series of repeated syllables and modulating
from a major key, to a minor key, to an orchestral silence out
of which a single voice emerges into song—a song that fuses
with the land since, like the land, it spirals on. The poem's
concluding implication is that even the moon is rounded by
our rounded mouths, which form a melody.

But we must be cautious not to consider "Evening without Angels" as representative of an enthusiastic testament in
Stevens's poems to the human condition. For example,
another poem, "The Pleasures of merely Circulating," despite
its apparent gaiety, has sinister undertones. Once again,
circularity is the dominant musical motif:

The garden flew round with the angel,
The angel flew round with the clouds,
And the clouds flew round and the clouds flew round
And the clouds flew round with the clouds.

Is there any secret in skulls,
The cattle skulls in the woods?
Do the drummers in black hoods
Rumble anything out of their drums?

> Mrs. Anderson's Swedish baby
> Might well have been German or Spanish,
> Yet that things go round and again go round
> Has rather a classical sound.

> (*CP*, 149–50)

The arbitrary occurrence of events that the poem considers suggests far more than a "classical sound." For as often as the circulating forms of nature swoop into a Chagall-like swirl of fancy, they also swoop downward to death. There are no secrets in skulls—the remains of the dead—and the black-hooded drummers rumble their own song of death as, for some, life goes on.

What is most important in "The Pleasures of merely Circulating" is that the music stands for feeling (alternating joy and a sense of foreboding) and that music is supple; even as the overriding tone is light, its undertones, less certain and hence formulated in questions, communicate dread and portentousness. Indeed, the circular music of the poems encompasses a range of feelings: in "Peter Quince," the dominant feeling is sensuality; in "Dance of the Macabre Mice," it is a subtle feeling of decay and mortality; in "Loneliness in Jersey City" and "The Place of the Solitaires," it is loneliness; and in "Mozart, 1935" it is a variety of feelings, each one modulating into the prevailing fact of death.

In the last-named poem, each articulated feeling is punctured by a "be thou," by a reminder that we are subject to the feelings that the great pianist's song embodies. Mozart, brought back from the dead, sits in rags at a piano. He plays "that lucid souvenir of the past," a concerto that touches the strings of humanity's collective soul.

> The divertimento;
> That airy dream of the future,
> The unclouded concerto . . .
> The snow is falling.
> Strike the piercing chord.

Be thou the voice,
Not you. Be thou, be thou
The voice of angry fear,
The voice of this besieging pain.

Be thou that wintry sound
As of the great wind howling,
By which sorrow is released,
Dismissed, absolved
In starry placating.

We may return to Mozart.
He was young, and we, we are old.
The snow is falling
And the streets are full of cries.
Be seated thou.

(*CP*, 132)

As he does in so many poems, Stevens uses a contrived character to talk about himself as poet. The poet's song, which is a pastiche of many of the composer's songs, reminds us of our mortality by stripping away the feelings that enable us to avoid it. Each circle takes a turn inward until the poem reaches its center—the place from which no one can turn.[17]

The feeling of death, which is a nearly constant presence is Stevens's poems, evokes two accompanying feelings, each usually expressed in circular patterns : terror and emptiness. The first is a dominant force in "Thirteen Ways of Looking at a Blackbird" and the prevailing force in "Domination of

17. "The House was Quiet and the World was Calm" (*CP*, 358) moves in essentially the same way as "Mozart, 1935." As we find Mozart seated at a piano both at the beginning and at the end of that poem, in "The House was Quiet" we find a reader leaning over a book. Throughout the poem he remains seated; but as the poem circles outward the reader and the book become one in a grand interplay of feelings. Yet, just as these feelings are mentioned, they are ripped aside. The poem circles inward to the point where it began.

Black," a poem in which the eerie presences of night circulate and confound in the memory.

> I heard the cry—the peacocks.
> Was it a cry against the twilight
> Or against the leaves themselves
> Turning in the wind,
> Turning as the flames
> Turned in the fire,
> Turning as the tails of the peacocks
> Turned in the loud fire,
> Loud as the hemlocks
> Full of the cry of the peacocks?
> Or was it a cry against the hemlocks?
>
> (*CP*, 9)

Here the circular motion is nearly claustrophobic; the details are few, and each takes on the properties of every other one, like a number of photographs superimposed on one another. At first it would appear that it is the cry of the peacocks, whistling across the night, that fills the listener with terror. But as the poem proceeds, it becomes obvious that the turning motion itself, which reaches from the leaves out to the planets, suggests an enormous scheme of gyrations that eludes the listener's control and understanding. At the poem's conclusion he admits that "I felt afraid/And I remembered the cry of the peacocks." The peacock's cry is simply one dramatic element of this enormous scheme— here, its reminder. The listener stands silent and terrified in the face of the night, baffled by a world too complex and intertwined to declare itself.

In this state of confusion, according to Stevens, an incomprehensible something is a companion to nothing. In "The Snow Man," which directly follows "Domination of Black" in *Harmonium*, the feeling of nothingness that forms out of the hard snow and the "misery in the sound of the wind" are most intense. For here, the music circles and modulates into a listener, the intelligence of his place, alone and empty. So much is this listener a part of his place, a person with a "mind of winter," that the barren, snow-blotted landscape makes him "nothing himself," beholding "Nothing that is not there and the nothing that is." Stevens's alternatives are clear: live in a land of variety and innuendo and its polyphonous sounds will fill the soul with terror and confusion; live in a land of single hue and tone, and its barrenness will fill the soul with emptiness. In either case, man stands as an alien on his soil unless the poet enters his domain to make a rich and ordered growth, an approximation of belief to reconcile us to the emptiness that is without.

In "Metamorphosis," a brief and grimly persistent poem, terror and emptiness combine in the natural decay that accompanies the winding out of autumn. Sister Bernetta Quinn, in a brilliant examination of this poem, suggests that its universe is a "surrealistic one, void of reason," a terrifying universe "where streetlamps are crazily pushed to and fro as if they were Villon's hanged men."[18] The leaves of September yellow; in October they fall. The music of September grows shrill in October. The circle moves inward.

18. Sister Bernetta Quinn's pungent comments on the poem must be quoted in full to be appreciated. She writes that "From the very start the wind is shown taking liberties with its autumn world, altering yellow to yillow as illustration of how September leaves lose their clear yellow to the brown stains of decay. Of summer, only the skeleton is left; the robin, symbol of summer, has migrated to Venezuela. At the end of stanza two, the sound of September is distorted by the wind to Oto - otu - bre; after evidences of seasonal change the word finally becomes Niz - nil - imbo, a blending of frozen, nil, and limbo, with of course a suggestion also of November. It is no shock to hear that leaves and rain fall, since this is their natural behavior, though the adjective rude as a modifier for leaves causes some surprise. But when the sky falls, to lie with the worms, one realizes that a meaningful universe where things happen according to expected patterns has been replaced by a surrealistic one, void of reason, as different as possible from things of August, a world where streetlamps are crazily pushed to and fro by the wind, as if they were Villon's hanged men. *Sewanee Review* 40, no. 2 (Spring 1952): 235–36.

By November, the music is a slow cadence of single notes issuing in the separate syllables "Niz—nil—imbo:" November, nil and limbo. Decline of place demands decline of mood. November is a limbo between the rapid and baffling changes of autumn and the emptiness of winter's single, pallid hue.

"Metamorphosis," like "Domination of Black" and "Mozart 1935," describes a world in the absence of the poet. In that way godless, and either chaotic or empty, it circulates into comprehensible form and substance for belief under the deft, transforming touch of the poet-hero. This is a point that "Notes toward a Supreme Fiction" makes quite clear, again by a great going round.

Part III of "Notes" expands on an aphorism in "Like Decorations in a Nigger Cemetery":

> Union of the weakest develops strength
> Not wisdom. Can all men, together, avenge
> One of the leaves that have fallen in autumn?
> But the wise man avenges by building his city in snow.
>
> (CP, 158)

The wise man rides with the changes in his environment. Rooted in his soil, he thrives on its fluctuations by anticipating them and becoming part of them. Part III of "Notes" depicts a series of celebrations, each epitomizing the union of man and his soil and the intertwining of their intelligences. Since these celebrations are emblems of the fictive process, however, they also partake of a distortion, "the more than rational distortion,/The fiction that results from feeling." The weddings are transformations, symbolic permutations of landscapes into human fancy. Thus the great captain who marries the maiden Bawda also marries the hill country of Catawba, where their union takes place. Ignoring heaven and hell, they join to meet the land. Feeling is, in Stevens's poems, precisely such a joining, a commendable distortion. And such feeling is concretized in the sensual swirl of "Notes."

Having depicted his celebrations, Stevens, in true pastoral fashion, invokes nature's creatures to proclaim their joy. They too engage in the poetical process, their various songs spinning the world into the transformed shapes of poetry:

> Whistle aloud, too weedy wren. I can
> Do all that angels can. I enjoy like them,
> Like all men besides, like men in light secluded,
>
> Enjoying angels. Whistle, forced bugler,
> That bugles for the mate, nearby the nest,
> Cock bugler, whistle and bugle and stop just short,
>
> Red robin, stop in your preludes, practicing
> Mere repetitions. These things at least comprise
> An occupation, an exercise, a work,
>
> A thing final in itself and therefore good:
> One of the vast repetitions final in
> Themselves and, therefore, good, the going round
>
> And round and round, the merely going round,
> Until merely going round is a final good,
> The way wine comes at a table in a wood.
>
> And we enjoy like men, the way a leaf
> Above the table spins its constant spin,
> So that we look at it with pleasure, look
>
> At it spinning its eccentric measure. Perhaps,
> The man-hero is not the exceptional monster,
> But he that of repetition is most master.
>
> (*CP*, 405–6)

Repetition is the poet's means of "getting at," a circling

around a particular object in order to gather its form from all possible perspectives. It is a summarizing of qualities, which is our best substitute for what we cannot have: final truth. In this canto, there is an Aristotelian notion not often found in Stevens: art is an imitation of nature. The birds and beasts are by virtue of their activities poets. Their turning, repeated sounds are approximations of their observations and feelings, just as poetical sounds are for the human imagination. And since these sounds can never reach and enfold a "subtle centre," they are in themselves a final goodness. What is most significant here is that the turning process is a natural one, a casual extension of feeling. Because of this, the "man-hero" is in no way "exceptional." He is only natural: a reflection of the operations of the external world and therefore the appropriate voice of transformation. The alliterative quality of the verses, of course, embodies the virtues of repetition since it creates a magnetic whirlpool in which all attracted phenomena get shaped into poetical form.

The circling process suggests some important attributes of Stevens's philosophical point of view. If we link this process to Stevens's overall understanding of reality, we can outline many of the tenets upon which his poetry is based:

(1)   Stevens rejects all notions of a fixed, stable reality. The external world is in a state of constant flux. Since we are part of this world, we can only affirm our orientation to it by flowing with its cyclical motions. Poetry is the ideal embodiment of such a flowing, because it both considers it as part of its subject matter and mirrors it in its form. While the poet can never meet nature, his mirroring is at least a persistent approach.

(2)   In the poet-hero there is no separation of body and intellect; indeed, there is no distinction between the two. For poetry is feeling, and feeling is a joining with the elusive moment in which the external world and the poem are one. Yet only man has feeling; nature

is vacant of this quality. Hence joining is not communion, but only creation, in which nature, transformed to correspond to human feeling, mirrors the poet's preoccupations.

(3) The poet's impulse to capture reality can never fade, since reality is different for him every day—at a new point along an infinite spiral. J. Hillis Miller has remarked on this point of view. He writes that, for Stevens, "[The present] evanescent as it is, is the only reality, and it is only in the moment, a moment which changes and evaporates with the utmost rapidity, that man can glimpse things as they are. Things exist only in the time they are moving from is to was." [19] Such moving becomes the formal substance of poetry. And he who is willing to become part of it is a hero, since he formulates no absolutes that would retard the infinite dynamics of the external world.

(4) Such a hero is "noble" and "capable," since he shows none of the weaknesses exhibited by those who search for naked truth. He realizes that there are no gods in nature, nor any sort of consciousness there. Yet he accepts nature for what it is. Were he to do otherwise he would merely be, as Miller puts it, like "a barren man in a barren land," [20] since nature could not correspond to the demands of his imagination.

(5) Nature itself is in no way idyllic. It is just as likely to have the ferocity of a lion as it is to have the gentleness of a lamb. The hero, moving with these fluctuations, is a violent as well as a pacific man. Since his craft is bloodless, however, it is a noble substitute for the baser instincts that produce physical violence.

(6) Even though Stevens contends that we live in a godless world where nothing is permanent, he does not ascribe to any position of existential absurdity, ennui, or *Welt-*

19. Pearce anthology, p. 153.
20. *Ibid.*, p. 144.

schmertz. He does believe, however, that the life of perception is futile and that poetry is futility's most lucid expression. Futility is a recognition that it is impossible to reach a final understanding of a world that changes constantly. But it is an occasion not only for terror and depression, but also for joy and celebration. The celebratory feeling derives from the knowledge that, if nothing is fixed, futility can be transformed into a realization of the world's infinite possibility to inspire poetical expression.

(7)   The function of poetry is "mere sound." But sound is repetition and a mirror of change—circular summary of nature. "Academic Discourse at Havana" considers this issue:

> Is the function of the poet here mere sound,
> Subtler than the ornatest prophecy,
> To stuff the ear? It causes him to make
> His infinite repetition and alloys
> Of pick of ebon, pick of halcyon.
> It weights him with nice logic for the prim.
> As part of nature he is part of us.
>
> (*CP,* 144)

Sound unites tangible reality with spirit, enabling each to change with nature. "Academic Discourse" transforms this unity into joyful celebration, a part of "An infinite incantation of our selves." Futility in the face of discovering that nature can never be fixed is also an enrichment, since it enables us to consider what we actually have: ourselves, looped along the various spirals of nature.

All of these tenets come into play in "Things of August," a poem that depicts the external world in the fervor of seasonal change.

III

"Things of August" communicates a sense of futility without any accompanying despair. It depicts the failure of the imagination to reach any sort of accord with nature. Richard Blessing neatly explains:

> The imagination encounters the world, but never the undistorted world. The moment of intersection is always a shade too brief, a matter of "was" rather than "is," a presence which the eye is never quick enough to catch. Life is composed of a series of such encounters. . . .[21]

The poem is "getting at" what continually eludes us. The scope of its reach is indicated by its imagery.

"Things of August" is controlled by a series of edges: the shell of an egg, the perihelion, the penumbra of a summer night, the edge of that same night. August is the furthest extenuation of nature into growth, the height of fruitfulness. It stands poised between growth and decay and plants in the mind the illusion that the world is momentarily fixed. The sentiments of the poet belie this illusion, however, and the poem is suffused with the awareness that September is a very pressing future.

As each day of August passes, the sun slants further away from the earth. The poet contemplates the past, which now stalks like a ghost through the shadowy intersection of the sun and sloping mountainside. But the past is only a "disused ambit of the soul," and the poet yearns for some way that the present and the future can collect about objects and give them a human significance. He begins to construct such a way by proposing a law of accumulation. Neither the noise of the locust nor the noise of the cricket is useless. Each is a "trying out," an approximation of the motions of

21. Richard Allen Blessing, *Wallace Stevens' "Whole Harmonium"* (Syracuse, N.Y., 1970), p. 156.

nature and therefore good, if for no other reason than because it is all that the cricket and the locust can have while
the grass begins to shrivel under them. The implication
here is that the only meaning in the world is the experience
of responding to it as it passes.

Yet, as the human imagination responds, it has the capacity to travel through several levels of realization. As Stevens
so often does, in "Things of August" he employs a meditative
process of moving through stages of understanding to depict
the active mind reaching out to capture nature.

> We make, although inside an egg,
> Variations on the words spread sail.
>
> The morning-glories grow in the egg.
> It is full of the myrrh and camphor of summer
>
> And Adirondack glittering. The cat hawks it
> And the hawk cats it and we say spread sail,
>
> Spread sail, we say spread white, spread way.
> The shell is a shore. The egg of the sea
>
> And the egg of the sky are in shells, in walls, in skins
> And the egg of the earth lies deep within an egg.
>
> Spread outward. Crack the round dome. Break through.
> Have liberty not as the air within a grave
>
> Or down a well. Breathe freedom, oh, my native,
> In the space of horizons that neither love nor hate.
>   (CP, 490)

This canto is an example of an old paradigm: the picture
within a picture within a picture, a paradigm that suggests
that the world is comprised of an infinite series of illusions.
But Stevens uses the paradigm in a unique way. He suggests that it represents an infinite sequence of realities. The

egg, of course, is the world, which is comprised of many smaller eggs. Like a chick, the imagination cracks them open. The stated wish in the poem is for a final shell through which the imagination can crack to see reality with perfect lucidity and with total freedom. Ironically, however, he who reaches this final stage of understanding finds a truth thick with futility. For the world into which he has cracked is indifferent. Its spaciousness, which presents an illusion of freedom, is neither more free nor more communicative than the speechless world he has left. Indeed, it is the very same world, and as usual, the poet must be self-reliant if he is to name it as it spins past him. The hypothetical mind of the canto has spun upward to see the world; but the world has spun by all the while the mind has made its grand effort.

Following his presentation of the ironic breakthrough, Stevens continues his poem in a dialectical fashion, alternately considering the will to fix reality and the acceptance of its continual change. Having reached the "shell" of reality at which earth and sky meet, he introduces symbols that define the furthest edge of perceptual experience: the moment when we feel such close kinship with nature that we mistake our observations of it for the objects that constitute it. The perihelion, the point at which the earth's orbit is closest to the sun, and the penumbra, the dark fringe around an eclipse, are themselves like eggshells, since they circumscribe the limits of the poet's reach while imposing an impediment to final understanding. The anxious mind, however, desires to break through perihelion and penumbra to observe the naked sun. It will fabricate false myth to achieve its goal, imagining that old and broken statues standing on the shore of the Mediterranean—the ruins of an ancient culture—fix the spirit of nature in artistic form.

The poet intrudes upon the musings of the hypothetical mind that he has presented. In a rather arbitrary shift of images that tends to upset the continuity of the poem, he moves from a consideration of statues and edges to a consideration of lilacs, using them to concoct an editorial directed toward those who would seek permanence in the realm of fleeting nature.

> The sad smell of lilacs—one remembered it,
> Not as the fragrance of Persephone,
> Nor of a widow Dooley,
> But as of an exhumation returned to earth,
>
> The rich earth, of its own self made rich,
> Fertile of its own leaves and days and wars,
> Of its brown wheat rapturous in the wind,
> The nature of its women in the air,
>
> The stern voices of its necessitous men,
> The chorus of those that wanted to live.
> This sentiment of the fatal is a part
> Of filial love.
>
> (*CP*, 491)

The love of the true sons and daughters of mother nature is a love of change and death. Once again Stevens resorts to the argument of accumulation to give meaning to the processes of change and death. Both enrich the earth; in effect, they allow the process of creation to proceed infinitely, since they signal a continual change of subject. The passage is distinctly Whitmanesque, an echo of "This Compost," a poem in which decay and death are the fertilizer of new growth.

Since the poem is the voice of a groping mind shuttling between a need for fixity and an acceptance of change, however, Stevens briefly turns Keatsian. Realizing the signs of August, he muses: "One wished there had been a season/ Longer and later, in which the lilacs opened/And spread about them a warmer, rosier odor" (*CP*, 491). The uncertain mind would like to find a soft spot in the perihelion, an extension of the summer's growth. But Stevens retards its wish. He turns to the rabbi, "Lucidity of his city, joy of his nation,/

The state of circumstance" (*CP*, 492). The rabbi, who is a familiar figure in Stevens's mythology, invariably represents a reality principle. He accepts "things as they are" with a serene wisdom; he reads the book of real things and, like the reader in "The House was Quiet and the World was Calm," he becomes the book: he inserts himself into things real and things changing. Like the couple lying on the grass to whom Stevens alludes at the close of the canto, he has "secretions of insight" that are mirrors of natural change.

The presence of the rabbi suggests to Stevens a concept of the operation of the imaginative mind. It is like a *tabula rasa*. The mind is a "blank meachanic," "possessed of sense, not the possessor." For such a mind, "the world images": it impresses its picture upon it. Yet the impression itself is not nature, but only its infertile reflection, as it is in "Anecdote of the Jar."

> He does not change the sea from crumpled tinfoil
> To chromatic crawler. But it is changed.
>
> He does not raise the rousing of fresh light
> On the sill, black-slatted eastward shutters.
>
> The woman is chosen but not by him,
> Among the endlessly emerging accords.
>
> The world? The inhuman as human? That which thinks not,
> Feels not, resembling thought, resembling feeling?
>
> It habituates him to the invisible,
> By its faculty of the exceptional,
>
> The faculty of ellipses and deviations,
> In which he exists but never as himself.
>
> (*CP*, 492–93)

Here Stevens depicts the mind in the first stage of a meditative process. Rather than shape the world at this point, it

merely reflects it. Since the mind cannot control the operations of the external world anyway, it may as well be open
to receive them in "endlessly emerging accords." But the
word *resembling* enters the poem as a signpost of the vital
transformations that occur once nature is impressed upon
the mind. For resembling is the poetic process of metaphor,
which habituates the thinker "to the invisible": that which
does not exist in nature, but which is its transformed image
shaped by the imagination. Resemblance is what is caught
by the imagination as nature passes by. Ellipses and devia-
tions replace perihelions and penumbras, since the mind,
far from reaching the outermost edge of the world, spins
randomly within it, magnetically attracting details and com-
pounding them to form. The person who engages in this
process never does so "as himself," because his self is part
of what is real. As imager of nature, he exerts his fictive
faculty, his hedge against despair.

At this point in the poem, Stevens has essentially con-
cluded his argument. He has established what he feels is the
relationship between the mind and what it perceives. Yet,
believing that a poem can embody what it postulates, he
must transmute ideas into feelings. The last four sections of
the poem are an attempt to confirm the validity of this
belief. Suddenly the hypothetical mind becomes a fully
active man. He is a noble rider, and like the hero of "Mrs.
Alfred Uraguay," he descends from on high, "From the spun
sky and the high and deadly view" to the center of reality,
"To the novels on the table,/The geraniums on the sill." He
understands that the "knowledge of things lay round but
unperceived," and so he sits "in the nature of his chair,"
in the immediate presence of things as they are, and feels
the "satisfactions of that transparent air." The dramatic
action, the choice of words and the final rhyme of the section
suggest that this noble rider will sit comfortably, enjoying
the pleasures of watching nature circulate, his mind circulating in a motion parallel to it.

Moreover, he is to sit in the poem as an exemplar. In the next stanza he is enlarged into "the wanderer,/The father, the ancestor, the bearded peer,/The total of human shadows bright as glass." He is the hero because he resembles all of humanity; inclusive, he is the embodiment of Stevens's grand ideal: the patient but magnetic man, whose mind is a gigantic glass reflecting things and circulating them into form. He is "the voice of union," the voice of assent to nature as it changes. As such, he is "A new text of the world," a courageous eye that excludes nothing, an eye like a rabbi's eye. This is not a magical eye; it can fix nothing and its possessor recognizes the futility in trying to do so. Yet it is

> A text of intelligent men
> At the centre of the unintelligible,
> As in a hermitage, for us to think,
> Writing and reading the rigid inscription.
>   (*CP*, 495)

Having created a hero and having handed him his text, Stevens can now conclude his poem. He acknowledges, without any further hesitation, the inevitable passing of summer into fall. The trees are losing their leaves and the world exhales "an odor of lateness." The "rex impolitur," the discourteous king, the snow, will soon rule "less than men/In less than nature." But simply because man and nature move in parallel designs, a snowscape cannot bring on despair. In any event, "the adult one," the mother whose children we are, "is still banded with a fulgor." She has given much to those who have accepted her offerings, and though tired, she will give more—enough, we are led to believe, that after winter's snow the spring will circle back to us, enriched, and veiled in new garments that will swoop too fast beyond the viewer's eye.

IV

Each of Stevens's volumes of poems, with the exception of The Rock, constitutes an urgent series of proofs that formulate the crucial belief that the world is dynamic, in a continual state of flux. Often, these proofs emerge from a system of opposites, or a shunting between two poles. For example, in "Notes toward a Supreme Fiction" Stevens presents the reader with two types of song. The first is the drunken, corrupt song of the wren, jay, and robin, an "idiot minstrelsy in rain." This drunken chorus sings a single phrase, "a single text," which molds itself into "granite monotony." Since the song is mindless and totally repetitive, it turns into a stone, turning its singers into stones as well. And since a stone is a stable monument, "It will end." Once we fasten objects to a single concept, the objects themselves begin to disintegrate, just as the hero who is commemorated by a statue finds the symbol of his heroism crumbling.

Opposed to this static song, which misrepresents nature, is the song that moves slightly aslant of total repetition, a song that spirals with a spiraling world. Perhaps Stevens's masterpiece in this mode is the third canto of "It Must Give Pleasure." Here Stevens depicts a world turned to stone in a repeated song; but he combats this process with his own rhetoric, thereby proving one thing while presenting something entirely different. He writes of "A lasting visage in a lasting bush,/A face of stone in an unending red." But he toys with the color red, following it through a series of changes and shifting from red-emerald to "red-slitted blue" to slate. Slowly we realize that the visage belongs to a statue, something meant to stand as a permanent representation of mankind. The ancient statue is worn, and Stevens takes advantage of this fact to exercise his mode of change. "The ancient forhead" now makes "channel slots of rain." He transforms the red face of the statue to "red-rose-red/And weathered," a model of resemblance and, as such, dynamic, since its analogues are infinite in number. From Stevens's construction, it is difficult for me to explain why he introduces the color ruby. I can only guess that ruby stands for the statue's eyes, or perhaps simply for a shade of red. In any event, what is important here is that Stevens portrays the ruby as "ruby-water-worn," uniting his terms to suggest the intimacy of various phenomena and their continual subjection to change. Through construction, then, Stevens undermines the initial desire for permanence that inspired the creation of the statue.

Having gained a rhetorical victory, Stevens exults in a spiraling change of events. Once again, he toys with the color red:

> Red-in-red repetitions never going
> Away, a little rusty, a little rouged,
> A little roughened and ruder, a crown
>
> The eye could not escape, a red renown
> Blowing itself upon the tedious ear.
>
> (*CP*, 399)

Each time red passes through the world it changes slightly (red, rusty red, red rouged, red roughened, red ruder), indicating that spiraling brings with it a new world each day, a world upon which the poet confers his devotions. The children, who appear at the end of the canto to see the sheep they love, scatter flowers over the ground, "no two alike." In Stevens's world, repetition is never redundancy. It is recurring action. But each recurrence brings with it changes, even if the changes are slight. Hence the "merely going round" is fundamental to the poet's style. Stevens, who "of repetition is most master," nearly meets the world along the circles of its own operations.

Such a frequent use of circularity indicates the intimacy, in Stevens's view, between the act of the poem and the actions of the world. But it was not until he wrote *The Rock* that Stevens could leave behind the dialectical method with which he presented this crucial observation. Evidently he felt certain, by the age of seventy-five, that he had reasoned out the futility of trying to fix nature and stop time and that he had shown how the mind of the capable man can briefly approach nature's motions as it stands among them. *The Rock,* as many scholars have observed,[22] is calmly meditative. It contains little of the immediacy or nervous wit of the earlier volumes; instead it softly affirms the poet's love of being able to come so near to nature itself, just as Penelope, in "The World as Meditation," loves her absent husband, Ulysses, who "kept coming constantly so near." The approach to an impossible meeting is the dominant subject of *The Rock.*

For Wallace Stevens, who is himself the dominant figure of *The Rock,* the approach is a vocation, activity enough to make a man. In "Note on Moonlight" Stevens is "Like a plain poet revolving in his mind/The sameness of the universe." The clear light of the moon discloses "the mere objectiveness of things," which gives the poet freedom enough to shape an infinity of worlds in the revolutions of his mind. Moreover, the play of nature fills the imaginative mind with a magnificent anticipation. For perhaps the moon, coy trickster that it is, protean conspirer of change, will reveal a

> figure waiting on the road
> An object the more, an undetermined form
> Between the slouchings of a gunman and a lover,
> A gesture in the dark, a fear one feels

22. Helen Vendler's afterword to *On Extended Wings,* Ralph J. Mills's essay entitled "Wallace Stevens: The Image of the Rock" anthologized in Boroff, and Richard Blessing's chapter, pp. 147–67 of *Whole Harmonium* contain, I believe, the most insightful comments on *The Rock* made to date.

In the great vistas of night air, that takes this form,
In the arbors that are if of a Saturn-star.
(CP, 531)

Each stanza of the poem unveils a similar pleasure in the act of merely seeing, of calmly watching nature change its face. But in the plain poet's mind, the night always provokes an "interior sound": the urging of the imagination to make the vast world into fictive form. And so at times the poet's mind, revolving, spins its shapes into the varied void. But even when the poet is silent, nature will perform for him continually:

The one moonlight, the various universe, intended
So much just to be seen—a purpose, empty
Perhaps, absurd perhaps, but at least a purpose,
Certain and ever more fresh. Ah! Certain, for sure . . .
(CP, 532)

4

A Tentative Introduction to Stevens's Symbology

For a number of reasons critics have considered Wallace Stevens a "private" poet. That he never claimed to be a spokesman for a generation, that he cannot readily be fixed to any particular school of poetry, that he rarely, indeed, identified himself as a poet, suggests that he stands as something of an anomaly in the world of literature. The claims of privacy, obscurantism, and indifference are convenient tags for justifying a cursory reading of, or ignoring completely, the works of such a poet. Conversely, they help to enable the zealous critic to stalk ravenously through an isolated patch of the poet's imaginative output, ignoring its surroundings while plundering the little space within for fact. He announces that he has elucidated the thoughts of the poet, while in reality he has done them two terrible injustices : he has tied them to a minor observation, giving false importance to a limited idea; or he has presumed to elucidate what is already quite clear. Having bent the poems to an unnatural shape, he must now show how they fit that shape.

Thus far I have tried to avoid such critical hazards by proposing theories capacious enough to contain all of the poems as they reflect the thinking of their author. And I have attempted, wherever useful, to give exegeses of entire poems rather than to extrapolate single lines and wed them to overview. But if Stevens is a private poet, whatever successes I have achieved in analysis will not account for his privacy or how it aids him in establishing his view of change, of heroism, or of poetry itself. For even the privacy of which I speak here—the privacy enjoyed by the mind as it peers into its imagined worlds of people, places, and things—is not inspired by viewpoint. Viewpoint, and indeed style, which Stevens believes are inseparable, are generic byproducts of a world within that words can only approximate. Since Stevens seems to have possessed an unusually complex and interesting world within, we need to lift the covers from style and theme and observe its naked rush of life to understand how style and theme in his poetry take their particular and unique shape.

For any man, we may write two biographies: the biography of his public life and the biography of his private one. For most people, Wallace Stevens was publicly a lawyer, insurance company executive, husband, father, and poet. But, like all men, he spent a good deal of his time within the confines of his imagination. From the activities of consciousness and unconscious cognition, his mind, like all minds, fashioned a personal universe. Some might call such a universe an outlet of escape from the ordeals of public life. Others might call it a play world, a place where one can influence life's operations in a way impossible in the public world. For the poet, this interior world, with its complex landscape, shows the features of a grand design. He plays in earnest. Unfulfilled in living with the random occurrences that constitute the life outside his mind, he uses the impulses and stimuli that appear within to form a stable, if growing world in which events take place in a way that satisfies personal expectations. As new stimuli bombard him from without, he accommodates them to his own interior world. This world in turn becomes more complex the more he experiences. But it always retains its basic design. It satisfies the poet's need for order.

For many writers, this design is so complex that their creations, even taken as a whole, reveal only some of its facets. For others, the design is submerged beneath a level of words that conceals it. For still others, however, the design dominates the writings to such a degree that the writings reveal something close to its entirety. Stevens stands among this third class of writers. He developed a very intricate interior world—not simply a world of ideas but one of specific people, places, and objects. Moreover, he developed a world in which he felt so comfortably at play that he could refer to it in nearly every poem that he wrote. Taken together, the poems are his private life, the life in activity when Stevens was alone with himself. In this life we find a wealth of characters, a varied landscape, and a series of sequential events. As we read the poems, we come to realize that this life is neither sporadic, nor whimsical, nor chaotic. Rather, it is continual, proceeds in a connecting chain of events, and reflects the ordering mind of the poet. Surely it is both more consistently and subtly ordered than the poet's public life. And for what it accomplished it deserves its own biography, a biography less uncertain than that of a person's public life, even if we include letters and records of personal relationships. This chapter is an outline for such a biography. I will write as a mapmaker plotting unfamiliar terrain, as a demographer charting the ranks of a population. In these ways I will mark the critical features of the poet's private world. We will see how carefully it was arranged, how smoothly and unremittingly it operates.

First, however, we must recognize the elements of which such a private life consists. And to do this, we must acknowledge an operant theory pertaining to the workings of the poetical imagination. I do not wish to propose a Coleridgean hierarchy for the various operations with which imaginative perception takes place. Nor do I wish to tackle the problem of archetypes, or collective unconscious experience, which one day may help to bring Stevens into a poetic community as yet unformed by critical standards. Instead, I prefer to show how a careful reading of Stevens's poems reveals a basic mind-set, or workable accumulation of data, from which the poems evolve. I am supposing here that the mind separates what it learns from the external world into two basic categories: that which is useful and that which is not. For the second category, the psychologist will tell us, the mind provides a warehouse, illimitable in space and oblivious of time. The mind, retentive of everything it perceives, simply renders its useless information temporarily inoperative. For the first category, on the other hand, the mind is a great sifter, parceling information into slots handy for ready reference as daily activities demand their use. The poet, naturally, calls upon whatever relevant information he has catalogued when constructing a poem.

Obviously, the parceling I have described has as its stimuli personal taste and personal feelings. How else can we account for Stevens's pervasive fascination with tropical flora, for example, even though he lived in the North? That he found palm trees of persistent interest is a useful fact for the reader and critic in establishing his imaginative mind-set, his private, which is to say his unique, world. Stevens uses palm trees as significant landmarks on his imaginative terrain. They constitute one of a number of recurrent details which, taken together, characterize the intricate world that the poems construct. And this world is not only private—developed from the demands of personal taste, which may be dictated by unconscious as well as conscious circumstances—but exclusive and complete as well. A maple tree would have no place in Stevens's private poetical world.

At this point the reader is probably contemplating a question that goes something like this: "I acknowledge that the mind is selective in the way that it uses the observations that it makes; but what will a concern for the fact that Stevens mentions palm trees but not maples add to my understanding of the poet or his poetry?" It will not tell us, I am sure, that Stevens was a connoisseur of palms any more than fishing references in Shakespeare's plays tells us that the playwright was a fisherman. It will add nothing to a public biography. But it will give us familiar referents that help to guide us through the poet's private world and the poems' public one.

I shall labor this issue a bit more. I have noted that the image of a lion recurs with notable frequency in Stevens's poems. As I familiarize myself with several of the poems, I realize that the lion, for which Stevens has so obvious an interest that he places it at accessible remove in his information storehouse, persistently represents a principle of violence. I realize, too, that this violence is connected to poetical expression rather than to physical conflict. Hence, as I reconstruct Stevens's private world, I can locate the lion in it and I can understand its particular function. In other words, I can see that this world, while self-contained, is also dynamic. Since it will always be before me, the poems having been written, I can understand its dynamics : I can grasp the nature and functions of Stevens's private world.

The purpose of this chapter is to outline the most salient features of this world. I will enumerate what I believe to be the most important symbols, or landscape details, that characterize Stevensland. Given the limits of space, my guide will be simplified. But it will also be sufficiently inclusive not only to aid the reader in his journey through a private world, but also to provide a tentative introduction for a further study of Stevens's symbology, which is the concrete framework on which the poems stand.

II

Description without Place

Stevens's poetical world is composed of a complex grid-work of words. It presents the illusion of place, but its chimeras are simply the poet's self-willed brush strokes. A daub of turpentine can smear a nation into wisps of paint.

> Description is revelation. It is not
> The thing described, nor false facsimile.
>
> It is an artificial thing that exists
> In its own seeming, plainly visible,
>
> Yet not too closely the double of our lives,
> Intenser than any actual life could be,
>
> A text we should be born that we might read,
> More explicit than the experience of sun
>
> And moon, the book of reconciliation,
> Book of a concept only possible
>
> In description, canon central in itself,
> The thesis of the plentifullest John.
>
> (*CP*, 344–45)

A poem is a "book of reconciliation." The poet, lodged among things real and tangible, fleshes forth his artificial fictions, drawing upon his surroundings only insofar as its elements cohere to his fictive visions. The product of his efforts is "intenser than any actual life could be" because it draws upon only those elements that fit his poetical shape. It distills diverse and divergent phenomena into a simplified whole. This product, the poet's text, is self-contained: it is a world complete with landscape. The landscape's features, which are interdependent, are words. We should be born to read this text because it comprises the experiences of a human imagination. Since what the imagination distills and consequently shapes distinguishes man from his environment, it symbolizes our distinctive human identity. Hence, description is "canon central in itself:" the condition of the imagination, which is the world as it is perceived only through the unique power of human understanding.

Thus, Stevens tells us, the "theory of description," which is the formation of a poetical word-world drawn from the random elements of the external world, "matters most." For "It is the theory of the world for those/For whom the word is the making of the world,/The buzzing world and lisping firmament." Being consistent with the hypothesis that poetry is a blooding of abstractions, Stevens makes his word-world speak. Discontented until he can give such a world character, however, he locates "Description without Place" in an imagined landscape drawn from a real one. He images a "hard hidalgo," a buoyant Spanish nobleman, who "lives in the mountainous character of his speech." For Stevens, it is immaterial whether or not his lusty Spaniard still inhabits his native environment. For his speech, a shaped, transformed manifestation of his birth soil, exudes the world of which he was once a part: his speech, which Stevens aptly calls "a seeming of the Spaniard," is a self-contained "style of life," a rugged mountain style locked in language.

For the perceiver of the external world, Stevens tells us in "Description without Place," things real exist only in an immediate present. Past and future are merely hypotheses; the past is colored by the imagination, the structure of which is words ("everything we say/Of the past is description without place"). The future is simply conjecture, the word-world thrown into the void of uncertainty, substitute for the placelessness of the incomprehensible not-yet-present. The immediate present, then, is for the poet a starting point, a center of vision from which ray out the seemings of the mind that form the fictive world. It is the point of origin, the place from which all placeless visions depart.

Since, as Stevens continually tells us, we must locate ourselves in what is real in order to draw fictions from it, he embeds in his poems ritualistic celebrations of the world from which the poet's mind departs. "The malady of the quotidian" is suffered only by the man whose pharynx is bad: the man who, failing to give voice in fiction, stands locked in a world of chaos and incomprehensibility. For the more vital of Stevens's poetic personages, the real inspires a fantastical voice to rise within them, singing the world into shape. In "Nomad Exquisite," for example, Stevens writes that

> As the immense dew of Florida
> Brings forth hymn after hymn
> From the beholder,
> Beholding all these green sides
> And gold sides of green sides,
>
> And blessed morning,
> Meet for the eye of the young alligator,
> And lightning colors
> So, in me, come flinging
> Forms, flames, and the flakes of flames.
>
> (*CP*, 95)

The natural elements, in Stevens's poems, are frequently given "a local habitation and a name." From these particulars, the beholder's voice rises in hymns, which are the imaginative response to the actual scene before him. The extent to which such hymns alter nature to fit the exigencies of the imagination is indicated in the poet's own response to the "dew of Florida." For him, the liquid cool summons "forms, flames, and the flakes of flames" as the dew explodes its sun-gilt reflections in his mind. He has created, in a sense, a speculated future landscape from an immediately present one: the storm that might generate from the tumid, dew-thick Florida air. As nomad, the poet has wandered from one world into another.

But his point of origin is external nature, the fount to which we come seeking inspiration for our fictions. We come, many of Stevens's poems suggest, as initiates, ritual-istically celebrating the place through which we will travel to achieve fictive shape. Stevens's "real" is a bountiful place, continually giving forth life, continually changing. It is fer-tile enough to meet any imagination, as florid and as multi-faceted as the tropical flora about which the poet often writes. It therefore naturally lends itself to rituals of spring rebirth, summer fruition, and fall harvest. But in Stevens's fictive world, these rituals are symbols: they acknowledge the real and thereby enable the initiate to pass beyond it into the realms of his fictions.

Two counter rituals help to explain the function of cele-bration as Stevens envisions it. The first occurs in "The Pediment of Appearance," a slight narrative poem in *Transport to Summer*. A group of young men enter some woods "Hunting for the great ornament, The pediment of Appear-ance." Though moving through the natural world, the young men seek the artificial, or pure form, believing that in dis-covering this pediment, this distillation of the real, they will also discover the "savage transparence," the rude source of human life. In Stevens's world, such a search is futile, since it is only through observing nature that one reaches beyond it to pure form. As if to demonstrate the degree to which the young men's search is misaligned, Stevens says of them that "they go crying/The world is myself, life is myself," believing that what surrounds them is immaterial. Such a proclamation is a cardinal violation of Stevens's principles of the imagination. For in "Notes toward a Supreme Fiction" he tells us that

> The first idea was not to shape the clouds
> In imitation. The clouds preceded us.
>
> There was a muddy centre before we breathed.
> There was a myth before the myth began,
> Venerable and articulate and complete.
>
> From this the poem springs: that we live in a place
> That is not our own and, much more, not ourselves
> And hard it is in spite of blazoned days.
>
> We are the mimics.
>
> > (*CP*, 383–84)

Believing that they are the life and not the mimics thereof, the world and not its fiction-forming imitators, these young men cannot find the savage transparence for which they are looking. In its place they find the pediment, a scowling rock that, far from being life's source, is symbol of the human delusion that there exists a "form alone," apart from "chains of circumstance."

A far more productive ritual occurs in "Sunday Morning." A rather different group of men from that in "The Pediment of Appearance" meets the fertile land in a more positive frame of mind. Willing to be a part of the "chains of circumstance," a single unit of the real instead of its embodiment, these men receive fulfillment for their ritualistic entry into "things as they are": a commingling of their blood and paradise, of the real and the imagined projection of it that a fiction forms.

> Supple and turbulent, a ring of men
> Shall chant in orgy on a summer morn
> Their boisterous devotion to the sun,
> Not as a god, but as a god might be,
> Naked among them, like a savage source.
> Their chant shall be a chant of paradise,

Out of their blood, returning to the sky;
And in their chant shall enter, voice by voice,
The windy lake wherein their lord delights,
The trees, like seraphim, and echoing hills,
That choir among themselves long afterward.
They shall know well the heavenly fellowship
Of men that perish and of summer morn.
And whence they came and whither they shall go
The dew upon their feet shall manifest.

(*CP*, 69–70)

This group of men finds the savage source. The process of the canto reflects the Stevensian gospel: forming shape from nature and returning to her breast. This group of men will always carry "the dew upon their feet," the sign that they derive their fictive form, their orgiastic chant, from nature rather than from any guiding absolute.

The ritual of praise, of the affirmation of the natural source, is a frequent occurrence in Stevens's cosmos. In fact, "Notes toward a Supreme Fiction" is a composition of rituals, each in its own way wedding the human mind and the external world. They occur as poems within poems, for the cast of characters living on Stevens's landscape is a cast of creators, each in some way reconciling his imagination and the life he perceives carrying on about him.

For the poet who creates his poets, ritual is a function of change occurring in a circular procession. As a poet of the seasons, Stevens can welcome each imagined spring with a new ritual, a new wedding of the mind to a new real. It is important to note here that for the poet the mind is a polygamous spouse, entering new relationships with each fresh perception. Poetry is not, for Stevens, a question of "final belief," but only of "believe": of accepting the condition of the temporary as the only reality of life. Because of its continually changing appearance, Stevens's landscape never takes on the characteristics of a Waste Land. Neither does the poet, unlike Eliot's anxious persona, wait for thunder or for rain. He makes do with what is before him at a given moment; and what is before him is always fertile, since the imagination never lacks the power to transform it.

Perhaps the distinguishing mark between Stevens and his contemporary Eliot is that the former points to the external world as the source, the inspirational root. For Stevens, then, nature is functional; for Eliot, it is incidental, convenient only insofar as its details serve as objective correlatives for the frame of mind informing his poems. This distinction becomes manifestly clear in a comparison of sections of a representative poem by each author. Both concern a rock, solidly placed in the center of a dry landscape. For Stevens, the poem "makes meanings of the rock." In the mind, "its barrenness becomes a thousand things/And so exists no more." In fact, in a peculiar irony that only a poet with Stevens's particular notion of the imagination's function could develop, the rock becomes the mind itself, shattered into such diamond-faceted brilliance that it encompasses all possibilities for human thought:

> The rock is the gray particular of man's life,
> The stone from which he rises, up-and-ho,
> The step to the bleaker depths of his descents . . .
>
> The rock is the stern particular of the air,
> The mirror of the planets, one by one,
> But through man's eye, their silent rhapsodist.
>
> Turquoise the rock, at odious evening bright
> With redness that sticks fast to evil dreams;
> The difficult rightness of half-risen day.
>
> The rock is the habitation of the whole,
> Its strength and measure, that which is near, point A
> In a perspective that begins again
>
> At B: the origin of the mango's rind.

> (CP, 528)

Stevens runs the rock through a gamut of human experiences, assigning its features to match the particulars of these experiences. Point of origin for the meanderings of the imagination, the rock becomes "the habitation of the whole"; it is the "savage source" of all creative energy. Stevens's choice of the rock as his prevailing symbol, here, is not an arbitrary one, for it represents stability, a prevailing center lodged in the mind, a node from which imaginative output can ray out and return, revitalizing as the seasons do to circular progressions of natural events.

In Eliot's "The Waste Land," the rock takes on a wholly different perspective. While Eliot, like Stevens, uses the rock as a symbol of the mind, he sees in it only a desiccative imagination, a water-starved impediment to thought, a hindrance to revelation. Like old Gerontion revealing his "thoughts of a dry brain in a dry season," the sullen narrator of "The Waste Land," brooding over his arid surroundings, speaks for the imagination's doom:

> Here there is no water but only rock
> Rock and no water and the sandy road
> The road winding above among the mountains
> Which are mountains of rock without water
> If there were water we should stop and drink
> Amongst the rock one cannot stop or think
> Sweat is dry and feet are in the sand
> If there were only water amongst the rock . . .
> (ll. 331–38)

Perhaps what most immediately strikes the readers of Eliot's verses is their remarkable similarity in method to those of Stevens. Both employ a kind of image building: a restatement of a single hypothesis, accomplished by a transposition of syntax or a new detail. The effect is a process of circular reasoning. Whereas Stevens's circling moves continually outward into fresh dimensions of imaginative thought, however, Eliot's remains in a single orbit; for him, only articulation is fresh; the mind dwells persistently on its own despair, issuing its monotonous chant to the dead land.

"The Waste Land" fixes on the mind's need, but also its accompanying inability, to conquer its own emptiness. Its tone, therefore, is desperate. "The Rock," on the other hand, fixes on the mind's preoccupation with things outside of itself, particularly that "subtle centre," that still point of existence around which earthly phenomena revolve to the glee of the creative imagination. For Stevens, then, the imaginative mind is firmly stationed in the external world which, possessing infinite capacity for change, freshens its beholder with each new face that it assumes. The major attribute of the productive poet is attentiveness, from which springs naturally a unique view of the commonplace, a nuance that sparks the ordinary into unusual, fresh life. Out of the most insignificant of events springs a flick of new thought,

> A flick which added to what was real and its vocabulary,
> The way some first thing coming into Northern trees
> Adds to them the whole vocabulary of the South,
> The way the earliest single light in the evening sky, in spring,
> Creates a fresh universe out of nothingness by adding itself,
> The way a look or touch reveals its unexpected magnitudes.
>
> (*CP*, 517)

Given Stevens's attitude toward the operations of external nature and the way they affect imaginative perception, it is little wonder that he makes his landscapes ring with rituals. For the poet they present, without the burden of a lecture, a demonstration of the uses of the fleeting present, a source from which the mind derives its fictions. The festival of innocence must occur again and again in the poems. The poet is the intransigent ineducable. He places no fixed standards on his art, nor does he expect to derive a final understanding from his observations. While each new poem is a "getting at," the subtle center that it moves toward shifts position as the earth dons new disguises. Every poem, then, is a celebration, each a new getting-at both an element of thought to add to the compendium of thought and an open admission of the innocence fresh facts bear forth from the human mind.

III

Forms of Farewell

Michel Benamou has proposed a few of the perimeters for Stevens's poems.[1] He locates them "between sun and moon," suggesting that the poems accrete from the tension between these two forces, each of which exerts a powerful pull on the poetic imagination. The problem for the critic is to locate and describe the function of both forces. Benamou insists that the sun is the "masculine self" and that the moon is the "earth spouse" to which man comes as bride-groom, seeking marriage to nature. This is a useful hypothesis, but it only begins to account for the complex typography of Stevens's landscape, which rests under the spell of both forces. For within what J. Hillis Miller calls "the infinitesimally brief flash between start and finish which is living reality," [2] lie all the nuances of seasonal change and tidal shifting that the poems consider. All these events occur amid the subtle luminescences that sun and moon bestow, and so each is endowed with unique properties that only a broad study of the poems can reveal.

Let us consider Benamou's perimeters a bit further. Suppose that in fact the sun is a masculine principle and that the poet is an Apollonian figure, chanting his ordering verses out of the chaos and complexity of earth, which is both

1. See Benamou's essay "Wallace Stevens and the Symbolist Imagination" in the Pearce anthology, p. 95.
2. J. Hillis Miller, the Pearce anthology, p. 15.

spouse and mother, like the moon.[3] Can such a chanter, in
his rage for order, bring his mother-bride to submission? [4]
Stevens's answer appears to be No, for just as nature plays
two roles, she shows two faces, each, it seems, at arbitrary
intervals in the poems. In fact, much of the dramatic tension
in them springs from the anticipation that comes from not
knowing which face she will show. Two short poems in
Ideas of Order illustrate nature as the great dissembler. The
first is "Meditation Celestial and Terrestrial:"

> The wild warblers are warbling in the jungle
> Of life and spring and of the lustrous inundations,
> Flood on flood, of our returning sun.
>
> Day after day, throughout the winter,
> We hardened ourselves to live by bluest reason
> In the world of wind and frost,
>
> And by will, unshaken and florid
> In mornings of angular ice,
> That passed beyond us through the narrow sky.
>
> But what are radiant season and radiant will
> To warblings early in the hilarious trees
> Of summer, the drunken mother?
>
> (*CP*, 123–24)

In the bleak cold of winter, we satisfy our need for summer
with "florid" imaginings.[5] Dissatisfied with things as they
are, we project our images of what summer might be. But
all our will to summer is a paltry thing compared to her

3. Even at this early point in the analysis, we must stop to consider
that these Appollonian chants have strongly dionysian characteristics. The
orgiastic chant of the ring of naked men in "Sunday Morning" is issued in
the name of rich complexity and not in the name of an idea of order.

4. I am aware of the Oedipus-incest suggestions here, but I prefer to
leave them alone.

5. See also "The Poems of our Climate," *CP*, 193–94.

actual face, which is quite a bit more radiant and alive than
anything we can summon in our minds.

Yet, while nature may be drunk with life, she may also
be alive with the whisperings of death. In her caprice, she
plants foreboding suggestions in the mind of the poet.

The Sun this March

The exceeding brightness of this early sun
Makes me conceive how dark I have become,

And re-illumines things that used to turn
To gold in broadest blue, and be a part

Of a turning spirit in an earlier self.
That, too, returns from out the winter's air,

Like an hallucination come to daze
The corner of the eye. Our element,

Cold is our element and winter's air
Brings voices as of lions coming down.

Oh, Rabbi, rabbi, fend my soul for me
And true savant of this dark nature be.
                    (*CP*, 133–34)

The rabbi, a stern figure who hunches through many of the
poems, reading the book of reality that is also the book of
death, can only initiate the speaker into the inevitable. The
shining of the sun is a reminder of time passing, the surest
symbol of death. The lion, another recurrent figure in the
poems, reminds the speaker that we return again and again,
as the seasons change, to the old violence in our souls, which
brings us to nature as antagonists. Fixed in a cold present,
unable to summon the "turning spirit in an earlier self," the
speaker awaits spring and mother nature as a bearer of
death.

In fact, for Stevens the mother-bride must be two-faced; she mirrors the imperfect paradise that is within us, which is comprised of thoughts that fly between the poles of life and death. These thoughts take on two basic characteristics in the poems, two forms of farewell. One farewell is purgative, a taking leave of the litter of images one creates in one's musings; the other is expressive, a taking leave of life, an abandonment of self to the swirl of the natural world. In "The Man on the Dump" Stevens piles up a heap of outworn poetic images and places the artist on top of the heap, as if perched on his own excrescences. This particular artist is curiously like the poet himself, for among the litter are a number of images that Stevens himself has used and will use again: creeping sun and creeping moon (the tireless day-night progression that so many of the poems entertain), the bouquet, the flowers wrapped in newspaper, the pears, the cat, the dew. As if disgusted with himself, the artist flings his litter about in saccharine self-parodies ("the flower-iest flowers dewed with the dewiest dew"). Yet

> Now, in the time of spring (azaleas, trilliums,
> Myrtle, viburnums, daffodils, blue phlox),
> Between that disgust and this, between the things
> That are on the dump (azaleas and so on)
> And those that will be (azaleas and so on),
> One feels the purifying change. One rejects
> The trash.
>
> (CP, 202)

One leaves behind him his pile of images to confront the naked self,[6] which later in the poem poses as the moon rising in an empty sky ("Everything is shed; and the moon comes up as the moon . . ."). One bids farewell to "stanza my stone," the twisting of elemental phenomena into com-

6. Helen Vendler convincingly argues that the "the" at the end of "The Man on the Dump" is the self one confronts when one leaves one's images behind. See her essay in the Pearce anthology, pp. 166–67.

plex poetical shapes, to reach the self that is the starting point of images. Curiously, then, this bidding adieu to the dump is one more festival of innocence. Purged of complexities, the self-mocking poet only returns to the source from which he will one day amuse himself with complexities once again.

Perhaps it is because of this paradox, which ultimately suggests that the poet is possessed of an irrepressibly squirming mind, that the assertions at the end of "The Man on the Dump" are so "qualified" [7] in rhetorical questions. As it happens, one of these questions—"Did the nightingale torture the ear,/Pack the heart and scratch the mind?"—which, like the others, is supposed to anticipate a thunderous "No!", could be answered with an uncertain "Yes." If we assume that Stevens's nightingale is as infectious as that of Keats,[8] that it cajoles the imagination with its skitterings, we can also assume that this poem of farewell, with its purging of images, will not move the poet to put aside his pen in order to uncover new facets of self.

In fact, the form of farewell as purge is purely hypothetical in Stevens's poems. That Stevens accepts it in theory is indicated by his preoccupation with it; that he accepts it in fact, that he can ever hope to achieve anything more than another "getting at," is doubtful. In several of the poems farewell is an ocean journey from South to North, from the equatorial lushness of the tropics to the spare land of North America. The prow of the ship must push continually against the lashing waves. But the sailors who bid farewell never reach their anticipated destination and so the poems save themselves from becoming horrendous clichés. But more significantly, the journeys themselves, the purgative process, are fraught with qualifications. In "The Comedian as the Letter C," Crispin, sailing northward, is

7. Helen Vendler's word throughout *On Extended Wings.*
8. Since the poem considers the images of other poets' work as well as Stevens' own, this is not a fatuous assumption.

tormented by inscrutable images. Though a hero in a small way, he is also the butt of the poet's big joke, which is the caprice of nature. In "Farewell to Florida," the poet narrates his own journey, his own supposed release from the clutches of equatorial luxuriance.

"Farewell to Florida" begins with an outrageous Homeric apostrophe. From there, it declines into ludicrous parodies of vocative verse:

> Go on, high ship, since now, upon the shore,
> The snake has left its skin upon the floor.
> Key West sank downward under massive clouds
> And silvers and green spread over the seas. The moon
> Is at the mast-head and the past is dead.
> Her mind will never speak to me again.
> I am free. High above the mast the moon
> Rides clear of her mind and the waves make a refrain
> Of this: that the snake has shed its skin upon
> The floor. Go on through the darkness. The waves fly back.
>
> (*CP*, 117)

Here it would be tenous at best to equate the moon and the feminine principle. The "her" of this stanza is the past, which is thick with the tropical foliage from which the speaker is departing (no doubt also the exfoliations of *Harmonium*). The moon is asexual, simply the unencumbered state of mind that the speaker hopes to achieve. It is the same moon that rises in "The Man on the Dump." It is the symbol of the mind as free from the burdens of the past.

The form of farewell as purge, however, does take its suspicious place between two of the essential pairs of perimeters that the poems outline: sun and moon, North and South. The past—"her mind"—has "bound me round," caught the speaker up in the circular motions of nature. By sailing northward, the speaker hopes to run a straight course out of nature and into the self—the quotidian of the everyday world, "a slime of men in crowds." He also hopes to shatter the darkness, to enter "the light of common day." And so, as if leaving an old lover, the speaker boards ship.

While sailing, he contemplates his North: his newer, purer lover:

> My North is leafless and lies in a wintry slime
> Both of men and clouds, a slime of men in crowds.
> The men are moving as the water moves,
> This darkened water cloven by sullen swells
> Against your sides, then shoving and slithering,
> The darkness shattered, turbulent with foam.
> To be free again, to return to the violent mind
> That is their mind, these men, and that will bind
> Me round, carry me, misty deck, carry me
> To the cold, go on, high ship, go on, plunge on.
>
> (CP, 118)

The parodic content of the poem's first stanza and the ambiguous content of this final stanza together suggest that Stevens has once more written a very qualified statement of farewell. The projected North is no more clear of complexity than the departed South (like the South, it will bind the poet round). In addition, the stanza concentrates most heavily on the journey itself, not its destination. Here we have a hint of Stevens's real priority: the motion toward, which is the creative output unleashed in the movement between two poles. It is little wonder, then, that the poem ends in suspension, the speaker's boat plunging forward on what seems to be an interminably vast sea. For it is precisely this will to motion, the will to make farewell a purge, that is the keynote of *Ideas of Order*. In that volume, Stevens is concerned with the shaping spirit, a force that, always grasping for the spare and simplified, draws nature into ordered form.

Stevens's persistent use of the farewell journey helps greatly to define the function of his landscape. Taken together, the poems comprise a teeming shuttling between sun and moon, North and South, winter and summer. Each pole is the extreme of its respective time, place and season. Between each pair of poles the poems surge to the conflicting magnetic pull. Hence, it is no surprise that, for example, Stevens's fruits are ripe fruits, since these distended ovaries bulge to the conflicting limits of new life and the onset of decay. Nor is it surprising that in the poems light is qualified by darkness and darkness by light.

In a delicate lyric from *The Auroras of Autumn,* Stevens poises his sentiments on the moment when summer reaches its fruition and fall whispers intimately its hints of a decline. He locates the poem "The Beginning" [9] in the same basic setting as Keats's ode "To Autumn," but a few days after. The sensuous woman/season of the harvest has lost the slightest bit of her glimmer.

> So summer comes in the end to these few stains
> And the rust and rot of the door through which she went.
>
> The house is empty. But here is where she sat
> To comb her dewy hair, a touchless light,
>
> Perplexed by its darker iridescences.
> This was the glass in which she used to look
>
> At the moment's being, without history,
> The self of summer perfectly perceived,
>
> And feel its country gayety and smile
> And be surprised and tremble, hand and lip.
>
> This is the chair from which she gathered up
> Her dress, the carefulest, commodious weave

9. Stevens tried much the same poem in *Parts of a World:* "The Dwarf" (*CP,* 208). Here, too, September stands between fruition and decline. As in "The Beginning," "The Dwarf" depicts that moment of waiting during which the "self of summer [is] perfectly perceived" while the first frost of Autumn clings to the "stubble."

Inwoven by a weaver to twelve bells . . .
The dress is lying, cast-off, on the floor.

Now, the first tutoyers of tragedy
Speak softly, to begin with, in the eaves.

(*CP*, 427–28)

It is Stevens, really, for whom this particular summer is "perfectly perceived": for the poem depicts nature in much of its subtlety: the darkness in light, the fall in summer. Moreover, his figure wore a dress interwoven "to twelve bells," fashioned at the moment poised between morning and afternoon, or one day and the next. The familiar tragic whispers,[10] which invade the house so inobtrusively, resolve the poem into motion from its still point lodged between fruition and decay.

In its slight way, "The Beginning" introduces Stevens's second form of farewell: the departure from life into death. Since for the poet "death is the mother of beauty," it is important for his readers to understand how his farewell into death produces so much of the life that his poems contain. Since *Auroras of Autumn* in particular considers "the sentiment of the fatal," which is "a part/Of filial love," the element of death in nature that inspires the poet to clutch her with the intricate evasions of his metaphors, we should focus on one of that volume's major poems in order to reach an understanding of this crucial form of farewell. "The Owl in the Sarcophagus" most conveniently suits this need.

Though not one of his longest, "The Owl and the Sarcophagus" is certainly one of Stevens's most cryptic poems. It offers a "mythology of modern death," but it also submerges its three mythological figures, sleep, peace, and

10. These "tutoyers" in "The Beginning" have their analogues in other poems. Consider, for example, the "be thou, be thou" of "Notes toward a Supreme Fiction," or the "keep you, keep you" of "The Owl in the Sarcophagus." Like the "tutoyers," these utterances are the first subtle whispers of death.

death, in a murky well of symbolism. Since the poem claims a mythical orientation, we can assume, as Miller does, that the owl is Minerva, the mind, which, having reached imaginative fulfillment, resides in a sarcophagus.[11] But while death is a presence in the poem, she exists mainly to inform the living of her influence on their imagination. "Death's own supremest images," the poem tells us, are living feelings: desire, will, and the activities of the mind itself. "The ear repeats/Without a voice, inventions of farewell." Consequently, death comes in the night, as a form of farewell, to satisfy the ear's craving and thereby to give the dreamer a sense of peace, which is like death in that the imagination has achieved whatever images it has tried to grasp and hence finds its work complete.

"Peace after death," the poem informs us, "is the brother of sleep," the embodiment of the illusion of work complete that sleep instills in us. Until its fourth section, "The Owl in the Sarcophagus" appears to be forthright. Death comes to the dreamer to remind him of the brief span of time he has on earth;

> And death cries quickly, in a flash of voice,
> Keep you, keep you, I am gone, oh keep you as
> My memory, is the mother of us all,
>
> The earthly mother and the mother of
> The dead.
>
> (*CP*, 432)

Once again we find expressed the notion that "death is the mother of beauty," an "earthly mother" who, in her fleeting farewell, reminds the dreamer of the meaning behind creative acts. When, in the poem's second section, a man walks "among the forms of thought," one senses that he is the

11. Miller in the Pearce anthology, 6. 152.

awakened dreamer, marveling and at the same time fearing these forms, which bear "resemblance" to the earth itself. He has awakened into poetry, as if taking the advice of mother death. Awake and walking through his forms, he comes upon sleep (at this point, the poem evokes the eerie sensation of a sleepwalker coming upon a dream), which is now an analogue to death in that it is "accomplished," exuding the "fulfilling air" of one who has ceased to produce images.

In the third section of the poem Stevens develops a conceit to characterize this deathlike sleep: white robings, which comprise "the ultimate intellect," creation fulfilled. But it is here that the poem moves into the realm of the cryptic and at the same time begins to reveal its central meanings. For, as at the beginning of the poem, Stevens has confounded sleep and death. He must return to peace, the intermediary force between these two, and he must build his conceit of the robings. In the process of accomplishing both tasks in the fourth section of the poem, Stevens builds what is perhaps the most intricate and convoluted edifice of words in *The Collected Poems*.

There peace, the godolphin and fellow, estranged, estranged,
Hewn in their middle as the beam of leaves,
The prince of shither-shade and tinsel lights,

Stood flourishing the world. The brilliant height
And hollow of him by its brilliance calmed,
Its brightness burned the way good solace seethes.

This was peace after death, the brother of sleep,
The inhuman brother so much like, so near,
Yet vested in a foreign absolute,

Adorned with cryptic stones and sliding shines
An immaculate personage in nothingness,
With the whole spirit sparkling in its cloth,

Generations of the imagination piled
In the manner of its stitchings, of its thread,
In the weaving round the wonder of its need,

And the first flowers upon it, an alphabet
By which to spell out holy doom and end,
A bee for the remembering of happiness.

Peace stood with our last blood adorned, last mind,
Damasked in the originals of green,
A thousand begettings of the broken bold.

This is that figure stationed at our end,
Always, in brilliance, fatal, final, formed
Out of our lives to keep us in our death,

To watch us in the summer of Cyclops
Underground, a king as candle by our beds
In a robe that is our glory as he guards.

(CP., 434–35)

Who is the "godolphin" and why is the godolphin peace?
Why is peace the prince? Why is he adorned with the
robings that were earlier those of sleep? How could he be
naked if he is also wearing these robings? Why are the
robings, once white, suddenly so intricately woven and
ornately decorated? Why does peace, the prince, "watch us
in the summer of Cyclops/Underground"?

The section's first stanza is a serious, elaborate pun.
"Godolphin" is, among other things I shall mention, Sidney
Godolphin, English Earl and first Minister to Queen Anne.
In the stanza he gets transformed into an impersonal noun.
But it is important to realize that Minister Godolphin was a
Tory, like his Queen, serving a Whig Parliament. He was,
it appears, a go-between, just as peace is an arbitrating force
between sleep and death. But since peace is not only
godolphin but prince, and since he is the prince of "tinsel
trees," of Christmas trees, he is also Christ who, crucified in

nakedness, wears the robes as a composite of the myths that have developed about him. In this context, godolphin may be separated into "god - dolphin," since early Christians accepted the dolphin as an emblem of Christ because it is a beneficent creature.[12] So the godolphin peace is Christ on his "beam," [13] who, "stationed at our end" in his magnificent robe-mythology of salvation, keeps our eyes averted from Hell. Like the Minister Godolphin, then, he is a go-between.

Such is the figurative, humorous level of Section Four. Stevens is contending with serious themes; yet it is little wonder, given his propensity to pun, that he would mockingly nail Christ to his crosspiece and in the process mock his own seriousness while reaching toward the prevailing idea of the poem. Stanzas two through six are not only a rich description of prince peace's robes, but also a swatch of historical criticism of poetry itself. For peace wears "Generations of the imagination piled/In the manner of its stitchings, of its thread. . . ." Peace, as intermediary of sleep and death, the force that intercepts the voice of farewell, is bedecked in all the images of all poems ever created and, as the image of the bee indicates, the natural processes

12. This last piece of information comes from an interminably long and infinitely resourceful book, Manley P. Hall's remarkable *The Secret Teachings of All Ages* (Los Angeles, Calif., 1962). Hall tackles still other emblematic functions of the dolphin, each, I suppose, pertinent in its own way to this section of "The Owl in the Sarcophagus." The following from Hall bears immediate relevance to the poem:

> The dolphin was accepted by the early Christians as an emblem of Christ, because the pagans had viewed this beautiful creature as a friend and benefactor of man. The heir to the throne of France, the *Dauphin,* may have secured his title from this ancient pagan symbol of the divine preservative power. The first advocates of Christianity likened converts to fishes, who at the time of baptism "returned again into the sea of Christ." (p. lxxxv)

13. Stevens toyed with the same image seventeen years earlier in "The Man with the Blue Guitar." In Canto XXX (see a study of this canto in chapter 1 of this book), the evolved man stands with his eye "A-cock at the cross-piece on a pole" (*CP,* 181).

from which these images emerge. So "damasked in the originals of green," the forms of nature, peace becomes the collective robe to which the images created out of an awareness of death adhere.

"The Owl in the Sarcophagus" ends, appropriately, "on the edges of oblivion." There, sleep, peace, and death meet once more in a quiet resolution of the creative spirit and the "mythology of modern death" is complete. Death is a form of farewell, as much as Christ, symbolically, is a form of belief. As death counteracts with life—symbolically, as Christ counteracts with the death of belief—the vital tension between these forces accretes as art. So we add to North and South, sun and moon, and summer and winter two more perimetric poles between which Stevens's landscape rises on the groundswell of his poetry.

IV

Music and Musician, Book and Reader

> I do not know which to prefer,
> The beauty of inflections
> Or the beauty of innuendoes,
> The blackbird whistling
> Or just after.
>
> (CP, 93)

Throughout his writing career, Stevens demonstrated an intense interest in the relationship between poetry and music. In many of the poems, the presence of music is simply incidental: "music" is synonymous with "sound," "note" is synonymous with "syllable." In still more, however, music is a vital part of the landscape. Stevens uses it to demonstrate the relationships between poetry and thought, poetry and feeling, and poetry and external nature. Poetry is infectious, Stevens tells us, and a number of the poems are dedicated to locating its affective power. Here music, at once palpable and ineffable, serves to explain the varieties of ways that poetry operates on both the creator's and the reader's imagination.

"Peter Quince at the Clavier" perhaps most persistently demonstrates the functional relationship of music and poetry. In that poem Stevens reveals his fondness for the drama. Although written well before the plays that appear in *Opus Posthumous,* it proposes the masque as a possible device for narrative poetry. The poem's second and third sections comprise a playlet which, stationed between two considerations of the relationship between poetry and feeling and poetry and death, offers a concrete example of how beauty operates on its beholders. This masque, which retains the mimic and musical conventions of its Elizabethan predecessors, uses cymbals, horns, and tambourines as dramatic accompaniment to the elders' bold invasion of Susanna's privacy.

Later in his career such fanfare was to become a staple of Stevens's often flamboyant style. He delights in bombastic invocations,[14] and the music of fanfare embodies and enhances the hortatory flourishes with which he introduces his personages. In "The Man with the Blue Guitar," even a rather paltry figure of death receives outrageous fanfare. In fact, the exaggerated rush of music serves to inundate death in its very vitality:

> Raise reddest columns. Toll a bell
> And clap the hollows full of tin.
>
> Throw papers in the streets, the wills
> Of the dead, majestic in their seals.
>
> And the beautiful trombones—behold
> The approach of him whom none believes,

14. "Call the roller of big cigars,/The muscular one . . . ," etc.

> Whom all believe that all believe,
> A pagan in a varnished car.
>
> Roll a drum upon the blue guitar.
>
> (*CP*, 170)

Like a campaigning politician, death enters the poem to the gaudy music of storefront heraldry.

In "Peter Quince at the Clavier," however, music takes on more significant functions than the mere welcoming on stage of Stevens's characters. For in that poem, "music is feeling" and "not sound": it is redolence, the sense of after-image experienced in the mind once phenomena perceived disappear. Music is a link between the immediate and the remembered. Hence Susanna's beauty registers eternally on the minds of the elders, though in a transformed way, and it resounds in her own soul as a testament to her spiritual purity and grace:

> Susanna's music touched the bawdy strings
> Of those white elders; but, escaping,
> Left only Death's ironic scraping.
> Now, in its immortality, it plays
> On the clear viol of her memory,
> And makes a constant sacrament of praise.
>
> (*CP*, 92)

Music, then, is a link between inflection and innuendo, its poetical essence the sustained bridge notes between experiences and their lasting effect on the imagination. Stevens's favorite word for this effect is "residuum," which is the totality of those feelings distilled and preserved from experience itself. Residuum has a sustaining power; its effect on the memory is to maintain its equipoise during empty seasons and barren years. Hence in "Autumn Refrain," for example, the southward migration of the birds leaves behind "some skreaking and skrittering residuum," which resides in the mind of the speaker to help sustain his affinity with summer. The birds' music is an affirmation of the real; it "grates" the "evasions of the nightingale"; it is more than metaphor; it is part of the "subtle centre" from which the poet derives metaphor. It is in this way that "music is feeling": it leaves behind it enough of the immediately sensed for the poet to create his metaphors despite the immediate barrenness of his surroundings.

Feeling, for Stevens, is more primitive than poetry which, in its evasions, is all elaboration of things immediately felt. Since music is feeling, it retains an elemental simplicity that poetry lacks. It brings us back to the savage source within us and so, like the form of farewell as purge, provides for a return to innocence, to a position from which nature can be freshly perceived. It is for this reason that "plain men in plain towns," Stevens tells us in "An Ordinary Evening in New Haven," seek appeasement in a savage voice; for

> in that cry they hear
> Themselves transposed, muted and comforted
>
> In a savage and subtle and simple harmony,
> A matching and mating of surprised accords,
> A responding to a diviner opposite.
>
> So lewd spring comes from winter's chastity.
> So, after summer, in the autumn air,
> Comes the cold volume of forgotten ghosts,
>
> But soothingly, with pleasant instruments,
> So that this cold, a children's tale of ice,
> Seems like a sheen of heat romanticized.
> (*CP*, 467–68)

The diviner opposite, here, is things poetical, against which the romantic illusion of harmonious accords battles in the human quest for simplicity and for a smooth transition from season to season. Such elementary diatonics later become the "Naked Alpha," the "infant A standing on infant legs," which opposes the complexities of "polymathic Z," the embellishment of poetry.[15] Music, then, is purge. From out the futile gettings-at of poetry, "Alpha continues to begin."

Music has its effect on what is primitive within us. Like feelings newly experienced, it is subarticulate. Unrefined, it figures in the poems as those primal utterances that precede the transformation of experience in verse. Musical notes, in turn, are syllables of the name of an experience realized only in name and not yet in the richness of perception that afterthought bestows upon it. It is in this way, for example, that the beautiful, "dark-syllabled" Semiramide moves, like a primitive archetypal feeling, through "Certain Phenomena of Sound."

"Certain Phenomena" is an exercise in three musical movements. The first is a primal song that "comes from the beating of the locust's wings" on Sunday, like the whisk of an afterthought beyond a busy week. This beating does not "meditate the world as it goes round": it does not elaborate into poetry. Instead, it is a simple sound "that time brings back," and under its monotonous influence old John Rocket, one of the multitude of figures that so inobtrusively appear and disappear in the poems, peacefully sleeps. The second movement concerns the chromatic and complex. The Redwood Roamer returns home from the woods to feast on the luscious mango and to recite "the most prolific narrative" of his adventures. Redwood Roamer is a Stevensian hero. He has bellowed through the forest in a voice "taller than the redwoods." He has stood in the midst of nature; now the sounds he makes tells of its complexity.

15. Compare these diatonics to the floridity of Lady Lowzen, that "bachelor of feen masquerie," who invigorates the old and the new "In glittering seven-colored changes." She is the spirit of poetry, of all the flamboyant evasions that poetry exhibits. She is "chromatic": her music is far more complex than that of the plain men who cry in a savage voice through "Ordinary Evening." See "Oak Leaves are Hands," CP, 272.

The third movement, whispered and chanted by Semiramide, is significantly different from the others. While sections one and two speak *about* music, section three is itself a musical piece. It proceeds as a sonata, complete with exposition, development, and recapitulation. The syllables of Eulalia, a lyrical and mellifluous name, float through the sonata as the outlines of its composition.

> Eulalia, I lounged on the hospital porch,
> On the east, sister and nun, and opened wide
> A parasol, which I had found, against
> The sun. The interior of a parasol,
> It is a kind of blank in which one sees.
> So seeing, I beheld you walking, white,
> Gold-shined by sun, perceiving as I saw
> That of that light Eulalia was the name.
> Then I, Semiramide, dark-syllabled,
> Contrasting our two names, considered speech.
> You were created of your name, the word
> Is that of which you were the personage.
> There is no life except in the word of it.
> I write *Semiramide* and in the script
> I am and have a being and play a part.
> You are that white Eulalia of the name.
>
> (*CP*, 287)

In this little sonata, Eulalia rises out of "eulogy" as a name for death. Semiramide (Semiramis), the beautiful mythical founder of Babylon, is dying. On the interior of her parasol, she sees the light that is Eulalia, which she enters as a name into a script that is her own name. And so Eulalia, the word for death, combines with Semiramide: death merges into light and Semiramide therein finds her eulogy.

The sonata begins and ends with the soft-syllabled word that flows through it. The word itself is light-syllabled music, the gentle sense of death that the sonata articulates in its notations. The sound of Eulalia makes music on Semir-

amide's spirit, just as the sound of the clavier makes music
on the spirit of Peter Quince. The sense of death that Semiramide experiences is primitive, a predecessor to poetic expression. It is all intimations, like the feelings music leaves
behind once it has stopped.

Music, then, is the poetry of the spirit, the primitive
utterance of a poem not yet ready to derive its shape from
the operations of nature. One can understand, then, why
Stevens wished to call his collected poems "The Whole of
Harmonium." Poetry is the refinement of sensations music
can capture before poetry itself can be born. Hence the
presence of music in poetry is its link to its primitive origins,
both the inspirational and the cohering principle that unites
a poem to him who creates it. "The Whole of Harmonium"
is the collective spirit of the poet and the pre-poems out of
which this spirit takes its shape.

As music links feeling and sound, reading a book links
nature and the reader. This is why we so often find the
rabbi hunched over his text. The mystical syllables that he
utters are the text of nature verbalized. This is why, too,
Phosphor "knows what it is that he expects" when he reads
a book by his own light: he knows that a text is a book of
nature, and that its pages are frames through which nature's
greenness reveals itself:

Phosphor Reading by his Own Light

It is difficult to read. The page is dark.
Yet he knows what it is that he expects.

The page is blank or a frame without a glass
Or a glass that is empty when he looks.

The greenness of night lies on the page and goes
Down deeply in the empty glass . . .

Look, realist, not knowing what you expect.
The green falls on you as you look,

Falls on and makes and gives, even a speech.
And you think that that is what you expect,

That elemental parent, the green night,
Teaching a fusky alphabet.

(*CP*, 267)

The line "And you think that that is what you expect" is not
only clumsy but also puzzling. It suggests that what the
realist will experience is different from what he expects. In
fact, however, it is precisely what he expects: the "fusky
alphabet" that emerges from the green night to teach him
that his text is nature. We have seen Stevens as a poet whose
landscape is composed of intermediaries—peace, music, and
poetry itself being three of the most significant. To these he
adds the book, the alphabet of nature methodized.[16]

Since Stevens fashions himself as a magician, a "sleight-
of-hand man" whose particular art is transformation, it is
little wonder that he delights in toying with his art to
capture moments when the reader, the book, and nature
combine. In "The House was Quiet and the World was
Calm," for example, "The reader became the book; and
summer night/Was like the conscious being of the book."
Since nature becomes the book it also becomes transformed,
having come to embody the meaning that the mind donates
to it. The poem proceeds in a circular fashion. It begins with
the reader and his book and reaches out to nature to discover the images with which the book is composed. When
it returns to the reader and the book, therefore, it has demonstrated how nature impinges on art and how, thereby, the
reader locates himself in "things as they are" by reading the
book. The book, an extension of man, is the intelligence of
its soil.

16. "Large Red Man Reading" is another poem in which a man reads
a book. The book becomes the "great blue tabulae" of nature, and when
people gather to hear the red man reading, they expect him to read "from
the poem of life." See *CP*, 423–24.

But, just as man is limited in his perceptions of nature by the speed with which nature passes him by, the book is limited by its pretense to a finality that the operations of the natural world easily defy. In "God is good. It is a Beautiful Night," Stevens once again enters as magician, facilely transforming a book into its scholar, the scholar into a musician, his musical monotone into a virtual symphony of the "great space" that the moon pierces in its travels around the earth.

> Look round, brown moon, brown bird, as you rise to fly,
> Look round at the head and zither
> On the ground.
>
> Look round you as you start to rise, brown moon,
> At the book and shoe, the rotted rose
> At the door.
>
> This was the place to which you came last night,
> Flew close to, flew to without rising away.
> Now, again,
>
> In your light, the head is speaking. It reads the book.
> It becomes the scholar again, seeking celestial
> Rendezvous,
>
> Picking thin music on the rustiest string,
> Squeezing the reddest fragrance from the stump
> Of summer.
>
> The venerable song falls from your fiery wings.
> The song of the great space of your age pierces
> The fresh night.
>
> (CP, 285)

This poem reflects Stevens's most pervasive theme: that the operations of nature are too swift and too complex for the perceiver to capture and embody them. The scholar, "picking thin music on the rustiest string," can at best respond to the magnificent chromatics of nature only with his paltry diatonic melody. His book, in turn, is only a meager condensation of elements too vast for it to encompass and contain. Nonetheless, its expressions are the closest that the scholar can come to his anticipated "celestial/Rendezvous."

But the poet, like the scholar who persistently reads and becomes his book, continues to push closer to what will only evade him. While pushing, however, he moves in that tense area between things imagined and things real. This area is Stevens's landscape, which operates to the opposing forces at its many poles. The landscape, of course, is the poetry itself. But that poetry is informed by several intermediary forces: the music that flows through it as feeling, the book that contains it as thought, and the peace that sustains it as beauty in the face of death. Behind it all, of course, is Stevens as hero, transforming the shapes that are nature to the shape of the mind while all that it cannot contain swirls on.

Conclusion

I must Create a System or be enslav'd
by another Man's.
                        —William Blake, "Jerusalem"

Large chunks of this book have endeavored to explicate
single lines of Stevens's poems. As a result, my attention to
them may seem in excess of my attention to generalizations,
to making vast and conclusive statements about the author
and his poetry, though I will not forgo the opportunity for
making such statements that conclusions to books provide.
Here I am in a bind created by Stevens himself. The poet
delights in paradox. He particularly enjoys presenting serious
ideas in the parcel of a joke, and his readers must tolerate
seemingly endless rhetorical flourishes to note the process of
a thought. As Stevens hoped he would, he engages his
readers in particulars. In doing so, however, he takes the
chance that his readers will lose the thrust of a poem's
whole. Perhaps he wanted them to do precisely that: to
forget that his themes are few, to focus on the little flourishes
that give the poems their vitality and fascination. This
master of repetition, with all his frankness, needed to create
the illusion of variety in order to arrest his readers' attention.
Possessing a mighty lexicon, he drew from its resources to
counteract the myopia of his thematic vision.

Perhaps this suggests Stevens's most pervasive paradox:
his frank admission of repetitiousness coupled with his obvious efforts to overcome it with what is at some times the

sheer vitality and at others the sheer doggedness of his poetry. This last quality—doggedness—is not one usually ascribed to Stevens. Most critics, myself included, point to his sly and subtle wit, his ability to find areas of resemblance in the most dissimilar of objects, his skills as a versifier, and his complicated allusions when trying to estimate his poetic achievement. All these facets of the author suggest his delicacy, his cleverness, his resourcefulness, and his brilliance. They mirror the poet's public image, particularly his refined tastes in wines and art and literature. In all these areas of his life, one might be tempted to say, we find a sensitive, almost precious man tastefully plucking the finest fruits of life's experience to fashion into glittering artistic gems. The single-mindedness of his thematic views, indeed, frees him for his delectable vocation.

Taken singly, the shorter poems, at least, do confer this image on the poet. It is an image that many of Stevens's earliest critics used to castigate both the poet and his poetry for social indifference and thematic frivolity. Understandably, though not forgivably, they mistook polish and refinement for a pose; they invented a dandiacal little figure of a man whose meager accomplishments would one day shrivel in the midst of his contemporaries' supposedly greater art. Ivor Winters, for example, in defense of his own rapacious humanism, held Stevens, whom he believed to be a hedonist, responsible for a retreat from the exalted literary ideals that he believed poetry should embody. Winters's criticism seems peculiar now—a bit smug, perhaps, and certainly moralistic —particularly since Stevens, as much as any poet of our century, articulated the ideals of an Arnoldian humanism, of poetry as a critical response to and evaluation of life, which is the foundation of Winters's critical position. Nonetheless, his was a popular response to Stevens's art, both as the poems appeared individually and as *Harmonium* and *Ideas of Order* appeared as volumes.

The critical posture toward Stevens has changed radically in the past twenty years, however. With the advantage of retrospect, the critics have begun to estimate the thrust of the collected poems, criticism, and letters. Fewer and fewer articles and books appear on individual poems or pervasive details within the collected works, while more and more endeavor to define the poet's general accomplishments. The recent books discuss "achievement" and "act," arguing that Stevens was on a resolute search for a poetical truth that did indeed evolve from committed imaginative acts that in turn were steps on the path to that truth. These books have succeeded in counteracting the narrow focus engendered by New Criticism's compulsive demand to hunt down every possible inference of a detail, every possible interpretation of an individual phrase or, in rare cases, a whole poem; but they may also have abdicated the critical responsibility to examine the poems' style, their particular mode of expression. While a book such as Helen Vendler's *On Extended Wings* has admirably and intelligently combined overview with careful exegesis, one such as Merle Brown's *The Poem as Act* (the title is surely significant here) is so persistent in combating the excesses of the New Criticism that it falters on excesses of its own. Words such as *act* and *achievement* are so monumental in the context of our existential age that they move the critic to an emotional exuberance that often flies right past the poems. Brown is simply so hysterical about the import of *act* that he confuses his own voluptuous and cloying responses to the poems with interpretation.

Yet the contemporary critical terminology that has formed around the poems is not without its usefulness. Stevens's doggedness, his determined effort to "tick," "tock," and "turn true" a few basic concerns about reality, dominates the poems as an act of commitment. Even the mildest objections to Stevens as a poet too facile and therefore somewhat frivolous with words seem inappropriate to the impression one receives from reading the collected poems. For upon such reading one realizes that he has confronted an intensely preoccupied man, one for whom a vast lexicon is a means for "getting at" those few crucial factors that establish a poet's domain in the world of nature, for whom each phrase is the slightest fraction of a one-degree turn of expression articulating a single idea. Stevens is, in fact, very much like his metaphorical lion, continually stalking about the object that commands his attention, continually trying new angles of vision. He is also Sisyphean, in a curious way a man of our times. He knows that he will never hit dead center; he knows, indeed, that his very occupation, the making of metaphors, keeps him off dead center. Yet he persistently tries to approach the mark that his art, warring with his understanding of nature, keeps him from reaching. This is his foremost *act*.

Such an act suggests another paradox in the collected poems. Not only is Stevens a master of the variety of repetition, but he is also a master at sustaining an intellectual duality. He willingly sets himself up as a modern Quixote, feverishly searching for physical truths that only empirical examination could reveal. Yet, like Quixote confronting a windmill with a sword, he approaches his task with the purely psychical weapon of metaphor. In doing so, he exalts the imagination's supremacy only to contend that what it accomplishes in the intensity of revelation is a "flip for the sun and the moon" to accomplish far more skillfully. He poses as a "sleight-of-hand man" magically transforming shapes as his imagination wills; yet his skill, he freely acknowledges, is easily superseded by the slightest shifting of natural light. He swells his figure of the transformer-poet to the dimensions of hero; yet he explodes this image with an allusion to nature's quick-change tricks.

It would seem, then, that as his own hero Stevens is a humble one, despite his obvious lexical gifts. He has created his own system of thought, elaborated in his very distinctive language. Yet he is willing not only to test it, but to watch it fail, against the infinite and cunning resources of the external world. If Stevens, as Helen Vendler proposes, has written a "duet with the undertaker" in "The Man with the Blue Guitar," he has also been willing to let his companion musician drown him out. The poet as hero is hero because he "propounds" nearly, it would seem, eternally. But he is never the "eventual victor," no matter how often he utters proclamations. He is adept in his own way, which is in-consequential in the face of nature; but he is persistent. Therein lies his heroism.

Therein, too, lies a need to redefine slightly the terms of the "achievement of Wallace Stevens" as he accomplished it through an "act of the mind." The popular critical position toward Stevens is that the poems arbitrate a conflict—all that I have written suggests that Stevens is a poet vitally concerned with conflict—between the imagination and the real world that is external to it. The "capable imagination" of Stevens, we often hear from the critics, tries to produce poetry from the tension arising out of that conflict. But I think we can be more specific: we can also say that the poems present the conflict between individual metaphors and the objects or phenomena that they attempt to charac-terize. The flowing beard is not the flowing river; the river does not depend for its motion on the presence of a black-bird. The relationships that poetry establishes do not exist in the world external to the imagination. They are the prod-uct of a mind. Each imaginative act of conciliation, then, is also a falsification. The poet, proclaiming that he is "a part of what is real," determinatedly absents himself from reality, all the while creating the illusion that he embodies it in verse. The poet as hero, claiming that he whips the world into shape, watches helplessly as it eludes him. For the con-flicts between metaphor and object and between vast con-ceits and objects are endless. Happily so, we must conclude from reading the collected poems, since the survival of poetry depends upon their perpetuation.

A person reading this concluding statement who was unfamiliar with the poetry of Wallace Stevens might decide that the poet was a dreary pathologist of imaginative futility. Yet, by virtue of still another paradox, we discover that in the poems the experience of futility is an occasion for delight. Stevens revitalized a long-lost art in poetry: poise. His poems reflect a pride in impeccable taste and in balance. Their enthusiasms are tempered by portentous innuendoes; their grim seriousness is undermined by ridiculous characters. The Crispins, Canon Aspirins, mad guitarists and lutenists, the Nanzia Nunzios, and the flagellants (fat flagellants, of course, since Stevens rarely abandons the poise of paradox) people a world of despair and death. Yet death itself can arrive with the gaudiest of fanfares. Stevens would call such paradoxes "elegance," his "ultimate elegance" being an "imagined land." But it is also poise, that stance of equanimity that enables him to draw from his most essential theme —futility—broad comic effects.

Poise enables Stevens as hero to become the object of his own jokes. It enables him to accomplish imaginative transformations and then laugh at their insignificance, to propose one theory and then undermine it with a conflicting one. It is because of poise that canto after canto of "Ordinary Evening" can exhaust itself, only to return to a fresh nuance of an old idea. For Stevens, then, poise is the substance that sustains his energy, that enables him to expose himself in all his serious absurdity as he performs his paltry transformations.

In fact, for Stevens poise is a matter of "believe." "Life is a bitter aspic," he tells us oxymoronically, paradoxically, a fragrance gone sour in the realization that there is no salvation in human misery. Yet, despite its bitter flavor, life is a matter of constant hungering. For the poet, the taste of words as they roll along the tongue provides the only satiation for this hunger. The poet is supreme epicure, sampling his delicacies of words feverishly since they are his only palatable experience, his only resource of "believe." Language creates its own sufficiency; but its effect, like that of a well-made aspic, soon wears off. The poet, however, sustains his need for new delectables by continually rolling out fresh images. Their poised articulation, set into a void, composes an edifice, a temple of "believe" for the otherwise nonbelieving poet. "The gaiety of language," then, "is our seigneur."

The man who dwells upon his bitterness, who cannot find comfort (or should I say "salvation"?) in a "well-made scene," despises the confections of the poet. But the poet retains his poise nonetheless. He is not only epicure but Epicurean; he possesses a tremendous tolerance of the void of which he is a part, the fleeting, incomprehensible reality that leaves behind his meek, imaginary forms. His small circumnavigations of things real draw frank attention to their relative insignificance. Yet he flaunts them as if they were stigmata lending men a sign of their identity. For out of such an exhibition of our incurable wound springs poetry : a landscape, as it were, dotted with monuments made of words. There is no element in nature too slight to supersede them. But in the world of the imagination, the building is a continual process.

Bibliography

Works by Wallace Stevens

Stevens, Wallace. *The Collected Poems of Wallace Stevens.* New York: Alfred A. Knopf, 1955.

——. *The Necessary Angel.* New York: Alfred A. Knopf, 1951.

——. *Opus Posthumous.* Edited by Samuel F. Morse. New York: Alfred A. Knopf, 1958.

Books and Articles on Wallace Stevens Referred to in Text

Benamou, Michel. *Wallace Stevens and the Symbolist Imagination.* Princeton: Princeton University Press, 1972.

Blessing, Richard Allen. *Wallace Stevens' "Whole Harmonium."* Syracuse, N.Y.: Syracuse University Press, 1970.

Boroff, Marie, ed. *Twentieth Century Views: Wallace Stevens.* Englewood Cliffs, N.J.: Prentice-Hall, Inc., 1963.

Brown, Ashley, and Haller, Robert S., eds., *The Achievement of Wallace Stevens.* Philadelphia: University of Pennsylvania Press, 1962.

Brown, Merle E. *The Poem as Act.* Detroit, Mich.: Wayne State University Press, 1970.

Buttel, Robert. *The Making of Harmonium.* Princeton, N.J.: Princeton University Press, 1967.

Morse, Samuel French. *Wallace Stevens: Poetry as Life.* New York: Alfred A. Knopf, 1970.

O'Connor, William Van. *The Shaping Spirit: A Study of Wallace Stevens.* Chicago: University of Chicago Press, 1950.

153

Pack, Robert. *Wallace Stevens: An Approach to his Poetry and Thought.* New York: Gordian Press, 1958.

Pearce, Roy Harvey and Miller, J. Hillis, eds., *The Act of the Mind: Essays on the Poetry of Wallace Stevens.* Baltimore, Md.: Johns Hopkins University Press, 1964.

Quinn, Sister Bernetta M. "Metamorphosis in Wallace Stevens." *The Sewanee Review* 60, no. 2 (Spring 1952): pp. 236–50.

Stern, Herbert J. *Wallace Stevens: Art of Uncertainty.* Ann Arbor, Mich.: University of Michigan Press, 1966.

Tyndall, William York. *Wallace Stevens.* Minneapolis, Minn.: Pamphlets on American Writers, Number 11, University of Minnesota Press, 1961.

Vendler, Helen H. *On Extended Wings: Wallace Stevens' Longer Poems.* Cambridge, Mass.: Harvard University Press, 1969.

Other Critical Sources Referred to in Text

Alvarez, A. *The Stewards of Excellence.* New York: Farrar, Strauss & Giroux, 1958.

Bateson, F. W. *English Poetry and the English Language.* Oxford: Oxford University Press, 1934.

Beach, Joseph Warren. *The Concept of Nature in Nineteenth-Century English Poetry.* New York: Macmillan & Co., 1936.

Brooks, Cleanth. *Modern Poetry and the Tradition.* Chapel Hill, N.C.: University of North Carolina Press, 1939.

Empson, William. *Some Versions of the Pastoral.* London: Norton's, 1935.

Hall, Manley P. *The Secret Teachings of All Ages.* Los Angeles, Calif.: Philosophical Research Society, 1962.

Miles, Josephine. *Pathetic Fallacy in the Nineteenth Century.* Berkeley, Calif.: University of California Press, Monograph Series, 1942.

Ransom, John Crowe. *The World's Body.* New York: Charles Scribner's Sons, 1938.

Sewell, Elizabeth. *The Human Metaphor*. South Bend, Ind.: Notre Dame University Press, 1964.

Background Readings (Not Referred to in Text)

Blackmur, R. P. *The Expense of Greatness*. New York: Arrow Editions, 1940.

Burke, Kenneth. *The Philosophy of Literary Form*. Baton Rouge, La.: Louisiana State University Press, 1941.

———. *A Grammar of Motives*. Englewood Cliffs. N.J.: Prentice-Hall, Inc., 1945.

Chomsky, Noam. *Language and Mind*. New York: Harcourt, Brace, Jovanovich, Inc., 1968, 1972.

Daiches, David. *Poetry and the Modern World*. Chicago: University of Chicago Press, 1940.

Miller, J. Hillis. *The Disappearance of God*. Cambridge, Mass.: Harvard University Press, 1963.

O'Connor, William Van. *Sense and Sensibility in Modern Poetry*. Chicago: University of Chicago Press, 1948.

Santayana, George. *Interpretations of Poetry and Religion*. New York: Charles Scribner's Sons, 1900.

Tate, Allen. *Reason in Madness*. New York: G. P. Putnam & Co., 1941.

Wheelwright, Philip. *Metaphor and Reality*. Bloomington, Ind.: Indiana University Press, 1962.

Wilson, Edmund, ed., *The Shock of Recognition*. New York: Doubleday-Doran & Co., 1943.

Winters, Ivor. *Primitivism and Decadence*. New York: Arrow Editions, 1937.

Index

Index to Stevens's Works

Poetry

Prose

P5